WJEC Eduqas GCSE
Sociology
Revision Guide

Kathryn Bowman
Steve Tivey

Illuminate
Publishing

Published in 2019 by Illuminate Publishing Limited, an imprint of Hodder Education, an Hachette UK Company, Carmelite House, 50 Victoria Embankment, London EC4Y 0DZ

Orders: Please visit www.illuminatepublishing.com or email sales@illuminatepublishing.com

British Library Cataloguing in Publication Data

A catalogue record for this book is available from the British Library

ISBN 978-1-911208-90-7

Printed by Printer Trento, Italy

04.22

The publisher's policy is to use papers that are natural, renewable and recyclable products made from wood grown in sustainable forests. The logging and manufacturing processes are expected to conform to the environmental regulations of the country of origin.

Editor: TAG Publishing Services

Cover design: Nigel Harriss

Text design: John Dickinson Graphic Design

Layout: John Dickinson Graphic Design

Front cover image: Konstantin Faraktinov / Shutterstock.com

Acknowledgements:

All images are Shutterstock unless otherwise stated.

p4 Taras Dubov; p5 tommaso79; p6 t DGLimages, l LineTale; p7 Shaun Jeffers / Shutterstock.com; p8 t ESB Professional, b Jarek Pajewski; p9 Evgeny Atamanenko; p10 t Wavebreakmedia, b Odua Images; p11 l Lolostock, r ABO PHOTOGRAPHY; p12 t Sarunyu L / Shutterstock.com, bl New Africa, br Pe3k / shutterstock.com; p14 Chronicle / Alamy Stock Photo; p15 EvgeniiAnd; p16 Vectorfusionart; p18 Radiokafka / Shutterstock.com; p19 Angela Matthews; p20 m ayelet-keshet, bl Drop of Light / Shutterstock.com; p21 MikeDotta; p22 Pathdoc; p23 Monkey Business Images; p24 M-SUR; p25 Lital Israeli; p26 Kichigin; p27 Wavebreakmedia; p28 Monkey Business Images; p29 Goodluz; p30 Rawpixel.com; p31 t Dotshock, b Yevhen Rehulian; p32 Office for National Statistics, All content is available under the Open Government Licence v3.0; p33 gerasimov_foto_174; p34 l wavebreakmedia, r vvvita; p35 Monkey Business Images; p36 George Rudy; p37 Elnur; p38 SUPERMAO; p39 Voyagerix; p40 Rob Hainer; p42 Bell Photography 423; p43 Magdalenagalkiewicz / Shutterstock.com; p44 l Iakov Filimonov, r Monkey Business Images; p46 De Visu; p47 t Lester Balajadia / Shutterstock.com, b Africa Studio; p48 Michaeljung; p49 Monkey Business Images; p52 DGLimages; p54 ProStockStudio; p55 both Monkey Business Images; p56 Sylvie Bouchard; p58 Piotr Swat / shutterstock.com; p59 m WindNight, b Sudowoodo; p60 l Sira Anamwong, r Natata / Shutterstock.com; p61 Nolte Lourens; p62 BadBrother; p63 Proxima Studio; p64 FrameStockFootages; p65 Ashva; p67 13FTStudio; p68 Aleutie; p69 Simon Booth; p71 m Feng Yu, b Monkey Business Images; p72 DJTaylor; p73 Nito; p74 Couperfield; p75 HASPhotos / Shutterstock.com; p77 m Robert Kneschke, b Robert F. Balazik; p78 Ink Drop; p79 Marcelo Ricardo Daros; p80 Boxthedog; p81 Nomad_Soul; p82 Hans Christiansson / Shutterstock.com; p83 somsak suwanput; p84 Ysbrand Cosijn; p85 1000 Words / Shutterstock.com; p86 AkulininaOlga; p87 Nuvolanevicata; p88 Serghei Starus; p89 pathdoc; p90 Taras Dubov; p91 tommaso79; p92 Stuart Monk / Shutterstock.com; p93 arloo; p94 Igor Sirbu; p95 Computer Earth; p96 Atstock Productions; p97 Etraveler; p98 Yeexin Richelle; p99 Neo Edmund; p100 Brendan Howard / Shutterstock.com; p101 Lukiyanova Natalia frenta; p102 Tero Vesalainen; p103 Irina Strelnikova; p104 Aleutie; p105 Pressmaster; p106 lamnee; p107 Arthimedes; p108 Rawpixel.com; p109 Alexander Raths; p111 lamnee; p112 Tribalium; p113 Olivier Le Moal; p115 t Ibreakstock, b Rawpixel.com; p116 dzmitry_2015; p117 umiko; p118 Tashatuvango; p119 Koldunov; p120 Chinnapong; p121 Monkey Business Images; p122 Smolaw; p124 wavebreakmedia.

Spec spotlight:
Highlights sections of the specification that will be covered on the double-page spread.

On the left-hand side of every double-page spread, we have provided the essential content for the topic.

Link to textbook:
Cross references back to the *WJEC Eduqas GCSE Sociology Student Book*, where you can revise key content in more detail.

AO2 Apply:
Where you can practise your ability to apply your knowledge.

Take it further:
Ideas and activities to develop and extend your knowledge.

90

Gender and crime

Spec spotlight

6.3 Patterns of criminal and deviant behaviour: patterns of criminal behaviour by gender

6.4 Sociological theories and explanations of deviance and criminal behaviour: conflict view of Feminism; social control, Heidensohn and female conformity, women and poverty including the work of Carlen, chivalry thesis

Link to textbook

pp 222–223: How does social control affect levels of female crime and deviance?

pp 224–225: How does poverty affect female crime and deviance?

pp 226–227: Are females treated fairly by the forces of social control

AO2 Apply

A newspaper article says that crime committed by females is on the increase. Explain why this could be happening using sociological terms.

Take it further

Find out whether female crime is on the increase or not in the last few years.

Stereotypes of the typical offender are usually male. Women are associated with certain crimes such as shoplifting.

Chapter 5 Crime and deviance

AO1 Description

Feminism

Women are far less likely to be arrested or convicted compared to men.	Crime statistics show that men are committing more crimes than women. There is a large difference between the numbers of males in prison compared to females. Only 5 per cent of prisoners in the UK in 2017 were female.
Women are more likely to be victims of certain crimes than men, particularly domestic abuse and sexual assault or harassment.	Women are more likely to be convicted of certain crimes including shoplifting but overall their offending rates are much lower. Men are more likely to be victims of an assault than women.
The way girls are socialised is believed to be a main reason for lower rates of female crime.	Traditional gender roles have socialised girls to be quiet and gentle. This type of personality does not fit with crime. On the other hand boys may be socialised to be tough, aggressive and to be risk takers, which behaviours are more likely to result in crime.
Women are also more closely controlled from childhood and even when they are adults.	Girls are not allowed as much freedom as boys to 'protect' themselves. Even as women they are subject to greater social control. For instance, women who do not conform to norms of being a 'good' woman may be sanctioned through the fear of gossip or name calling. This keeps many women in check.

Sociological concepts, gender and crime

Women were ignored by many criminologists. Otto Pollak was one of the first to develop ideas about female crime.	Pollak developed the 'chivalry thesis', which is the idea that women are not punished as harshly by the agents of social control from teachers to judges and the police who feel sorry for women who get into trouble and go easy on them. This accounts for all the extra men in prison, according to this view.
Frances Heidensohn developed the idea that women live in a male-controlled world and must conform to society's expectations.	According to Heidensohn, we live in a patriarchy and women have to behave according to the norms of their role. Women get less opportunity because they have fewer opportunities to commit crime as there is such great social control over them.
A different view is that of the demonisation of women.	This view states that women are treated more harshly by the forces of social control for certain crimes. Women who commit crimes which do not fit with ideas about how a women or mother should behave are treated especially harshly by the media. They are demonised for crimes involving any aspect of cruelty in a way that a man would not be.
Violent crime is linked closely to men.	This is often linked to ideas about masculinity. Men are expected to be aggressive and tough and violence can fit with this. The crisis of masculinity may mean that some men need to 'prove' their masculinity in other ways even more if they cannot prove it through being a breadwinner.

The information on the right-hand side of the page offers ideas for evaluation to ensure you know what you need to achieve the highest grades.

Evaluation

Gender and crime   91

Strengths of the chivalry thesis are:

There are much greater numbers of male arrests, convictions and a vastly greater percentage of men are in prison.

The thesis may not be completely true, yet it was an important study as it started off the study of female crime. Even though it was written by a man it was a step forward and started the debate.

The view of different treatment of boys at school traditionally may have some merit. Women may also be treated more leniently if they are pregnant or already mothers.

Weaknesses of the chivalry thesis are:

The original study by Pollak was not based on evidence.

It acts as an excuse for male crime and tries to say that men are not as guilty as it appears.

Pollak's view that women were better at hiding their crimes was not really backed up with any evidence for this and just suited his theory.

Strengths of the theory of the demonisation of women are:

This theory challenges the chivalry thesis. Women are treated worse than men, especially by the media, if they are guilty of some crimes.

There are lots of examples of the demonisation of women in the media. Myra Hindley, Rose West and Maxine Carr are examples of this.

Pat Carlen suggests that courts treat women worse if they do not fit the gender stereotype of good mother and housewife.

Weaknesses of the theory of the demonisation of women are:

The cases where women are demonised are extreme cases.

Lower numbers of females in prisons may suggest that women are less likely to be convicted and sent to prison.

Men who commit crimes involving cruelty are also demonised. However, there are fewer women involved in such crimes.

Sociologists say that there has been a crisis of masculinity for young men who are shut out from their traditional role of breadwinner. There has also been a decline in traditional masculine manual jobs.

REVISION BOOSTER

Answers to questions on gender and crime often only refer to women. Refer to evidence, studies and histories of men as well as women.

Key figure

Pat Carlen is an essential figure to know; she tried to explain why some women do turn to crime. Women are more likely to live in poverty for a variety of reasons including low pay and being a single parent.

Carlen interviewed and observed a group of 39 women aged between 15 and 46. Her research was qualitative, and she found that crime had a range of meanings for women. Some turned to crime for excitement and others because of problems they had with drugs and alcohol.

Think link

This topic links closely to stratification and life-chances. It also links to the family and ideas about traditional gender roles.

Knowledge check

1. Identify two ways in which social control may be stricter for females.   **(2 marks)**

2. 'Females are treated less harshly by the police and courts.' Do you agree?   **(15 marks)**

Revision Booster: Invaluable advice to help you prepare for assessment.

Key figure: Highlights the key figures you must know for each component.

Think link: Encourages you to view the topics holistically and consider how they link with each other.

Knowledge check: Questions to test your sociological knowledge and understanding, and practise the skills you need for the written exams.

Spec spotlight

1.1 Key sociological concepts: culture, norms, values, roles, status, identity, sanctions

Link to textbook
pp 10–13: Key sociological concepts

AO2 Apply

Imagine you were writing a travel guide for England. Think about what you would include about English culture – what makes it unique? Think of all the characteristics that make up culture and give examples for each one. Ask your family and friends – do they agree with the examples you have given? Would they include something different to explain English culture?

What would you include in a travel guide to England?

Take it further

Jemimah Wright spent time studying the Yanomami tribe in the Amazon and found many differences in norms and values between the UK and themselves in how they regard babies, disabilities and multiple births. Read some of her findings to explain how norms and values vary between cultures.

What makes culture?

There are many things that make up 'culture'. These include food, language, clothing, religion, music, history, art, customs, knowledge, skills, values, beliefs, roles, norms and rules.

Afternoon tea was introduced to England in the 1840s and is now very much a part of British culture.

Culture	Shared way of life of a group of people. It includes norms, beliefs, values and language.
Cultural relativity	The idea that what is normal in one culture is different in another.
Cultural universal	Social behaviours that can be found in all cultures.
Norms	Expected behaviour in a particular situation or culture/social rules for correct behaviour. For example, how to eat with a knife and a fork.
Values	Shared beliefs that societies see as important and worthwhile. More generalised beliefs and goals about how to behave. Powerful beliefs that most people agree on.
Morals	Ideas about what behaviour is right and wrong.
Roles	Expected behaviour or part played by someone in a particular situation.
Role model	Someone who is respected or looked up to by others.
Status	Respect others give to you in society. Your position in society.
Identity	How we see ourselves and how others see us.

How are norms and values transmitted?

School	Family
Durkheim saw one of the main functions of education as passing on society's norms and values.	Children imitate family members.
Formal social control – discipline within lessons and by staff.	Children are rewarded for socially acceptable behaviour.
Informal social control – peer group pressure.	Children are punished for socially deviant behaviour.
	G.P. Murdock believes that the family passes on society's norms and values to the next generation.

Peer group	Media
A child or young person's peer group (friends, people of a similar age) is a secondary agent of socialisation. The peer group might have its own norms and values and so influence its members' choices of clothes, music and behaviour as the individual conforms to fit in.	The media (television, newspapers, magazines, websites including social media, radio, etc.) is another secondary agent of socialisation. Children in particular are influenced by the role models they see in the media and may copy their behaviour. The media can also influence the way people think about certain groups by the way it presents and labels them.

Are norms learnt through primary socialisation?

The family is the main agent of primary socialisation. This is how the norms and values of society are internalised.

Gender norms are learnt in the family through canalisation and manipulation.

Norms related to ethnicity are learnt within the family. Ghuman found that first generation Asian parents socialised their children into Asian values rather than British values.

Socialisation continues throughout life

Norms are also learnt through agencies of secondary socialisation.

Secondary socialisation teaches us that the norms we learnt from our families may need to be adapted as we encounter new situations.

Norms learnt at home may have to change as society and times change.

Values

Values refer to what is considered worthwhile and worth working to achieve in a society. Like norms, values are learned and shared. Our values influence how we behave. Our norms will indicate what behaviour is acceptable to achieve what we value. Sometimes, people might be socialised into values that are not easy to achieve and so might break the accepted norms to reach the goal, for example an unemployed person who steals to acquire the latest smartphone.

REVISION BOOSTER

Status is your position in society and the respect others give to you. Status can be either ascribed or achieved. Ascribed status is fixed at birth and is because of something you cannot change. You are born into this social position. An example of ascribed status is the Queen, as she inherited her status from her father when he died. Achieved status is earnt through education and work and is based on merit, skills and abilities. Being a professional athlete or the manager of a large company or being promoted at work are examples of achieved status. This is a concept developed by Ralph Linton.

The Queen is an example of ascribed status.

REVISION BOOSTER

Remember there are no AO3 marks for this section of the course so you will not be asked to discuss/evaluate any of the concepts. You must be able to describe and explain them.

Key figure

Ralph Linton describes culture as the way of life shared by members of a society which they pass from generation to generation. It is learnt and without it, he believes, there is no human society.

Think link

Although this revision spread is about key concepts of sociology, try to also think of ways of bringing in what you have learnt about primary and secondary socialisation, the nature/nurture debate and feral children and how they are linked.

Knowledge check

1. Describe what is meant by culture. **(2 marks)**
2. Describe what is meant by cultural diversity. **(2 marks)**
3. Explain how norms are learnt through primary socialisation. **(4 marks)**
4. Explain how status can be achieved. **(4 marks)**

Spec spotlight

1.2 Debates over the acquisition of identity: nature/nurture

1.2 Debates over the acquisition of identity: cultural diversity

Link to textbook

AO2 Apply

Edik was found in Ukraine in an apartment in 1999. He had been raised by dogs and lived in poverty. What did researchers learn about nature versus nurture from the case of Edik? How is the case of Edik similar to and different to the case of Oxana Malaya?

Take it further

There are many differences in what religious believers believe about the god they worship and the way in which they worship their deity. Make a list of the differences in the beliefs and practices of Christians, Muslims and Jews. How can these be used in a question on cultural diversity or nurture theory?

People from different cultures around the world eat different foods. This is one aspect of cultural diversity.

The nature versus nurture debate hinges around the discussion about whether our behaviour is predetermined and caused by our genetics and DNA or if it is learnt and is the result of environmental factors. Psychologists tend to lean towards the nature theories while sociologists tend to agree with nurture. The nature/nurture discussion is a complex issue and most people would argue that it is very difficult to give a definitive answer to the question. Many people agree that nature and nurture work together and the debate is in fact about which is the best explanation or has the biggest influence. You are studying sociology and you need to be aware that sociologists tend to support nurture theories and believe that they are more significant.

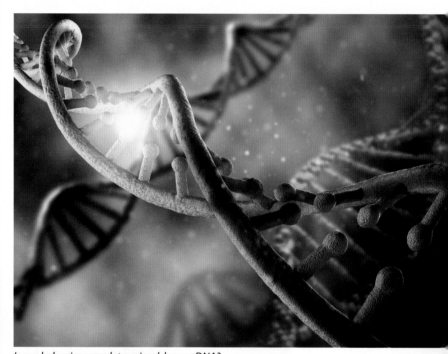

Is our behaviour predetermined by our DNA?

Cultural diversity:	Cultural diversity is the difference between cultures around the world. People in different cultures follow different rules and have different norms and values.
How does cultural diversity support nurture theory?	The range of different cultures that exist, for example, the different foods that people eat, the different clothes people wear, the different languages people speak and the different religions they follow suggest that behaviour is learnt rather than innate. If this behaviour was innate then there would not be so many differences around the world.

Nature theory:	Nurture theory:
Our behaviour is innate/natural.	Our behaviour is learnt from agencies of socialisation (such as the family) and is the result of our upbringing in society. It is down to our social environment.
Instincts are evidence that some behaviour is innate.	Feral children do not naturally have basic skills and therefore must be taught them – for example Oxana Malaya and Genie Wiley.
Some behaviour is part of our genetic make up/ DNA. Our behaviour is predetermined by our genes.	Cultural diversity shows that cultures are different all over the world and so people must learn their culture.
Twins often share the same characteristics.	Human behaviour has changed over time and throughout history.
This argument is generally put forward by biologists and some psychologists.	This argument is generally put forward by sociologists.
Most animals with the same genes look and behave in the same way.	Women are supposed to have a maternal instinct yet some mothers abuse or abandon their babies.
Scientists suggest we inherit behaviour traits from our parents, just as we do hair colour.	Some people die by suicide which goes against the idea that we have an innate drive to keep ourselves alive.
The example of the Jim Twins.	The case of Edik in Ukraine.
There is a link between testosterone and aggressive behaviour – female rats who were given extra testosterone after both were more aggressive than other female rats who were not given the same doses of testosterone.	

Ann Oakley believes that roles such as housewives are learnt and the result of nurture.

Spec spotlight

1.3 The process of socialisation: agents of socialisation (family)

Link to textbook
pp 16–17: Socialisation

AO2 Apply

Think about your own upbringing and socialisation. Who or what has influenced you, your beliefs, your identity and your understanding of your culture, your ethnicity and your nationality? Who or what has been the biggest influence? Why do you believe that they have been the most influential?

Take it further

Genie Wiley was found in California in the 1970s and is a well-known example to use when studying the nature versus nurture debate and feral children. She was found aged 13 strapped to a potty chair. Research her story: in what conditions was she found, what happened after she was found and what did the scientists who worked with her find out about human development and primary socialisation?

Key figure

Talcott Parsons said that the family is one of the most important and basic institutions during primary socialisation as it teaches children the norms and values of their culture and prepares them for adulthood. Parsons believes that without the family socialising their children, they will be unable to participate in society later on in life. This is because they won't have internalised the appropriate norms and values or learnt the basics of their culture.

Socialisation is the process of learning the expected rules, norms and values of a culture.

What is primary socialisation?

The family is a child's first social group so that is where the earliest learning, or primary socialisation, takes place. It is an ongoing process that takes place within a family and continues throughout life and is where we are taught attitudes, skills, knowledge, norms and values by our family. It is how children learn how to behave and what to believe and is important because we can't function in society without it.

Primary socialisation takes place within the family.

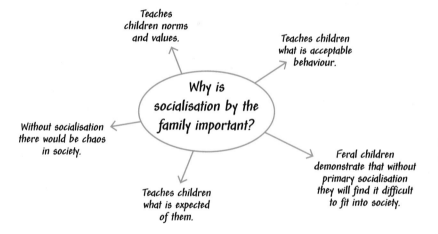

Teaches children norms and values.

Teaches children what is acceptable behaviour.

Why is socialisation by the family important?

Without socialisation there would be chaos in society.

Feral children demonstrate that without primary socialisation they will find it difficult to fit into society.

Teaches children what is expected of them.

How do children learn society's norms and values through primary socialisation?

The family is the main agency of primary socialisation and, as such, children learn norms associated with their culture as well as their gender, ethnicity, nationality, age and social class. Children learn these norms and values through manipulation (parents control their behaviour), canalisation (and direct children into certain interests, toys, etc.), negative and positive sanctions (rewards and punishments), verbal appellations (e.g. 'good girl', 'strong boy'), role modelling and imitation (copying their parents).

Children learn norms and values from their parents who act as role models.

Primary socialisation is very important in the early years:

Feral children, such as Oxana Malaya, cannot fit into society as they have never learnt the basic norms and values.

Children will often imitate the adults around them and accept the norms and values they are shown.

If you don't have the basics (language, how to walk, manners, hygiene, etc.) then people will find it difficult to move onto secondary socialisation.

As the child gets older, other agents of socialisation become important:

The family may become less influential as you grow older and are also influenced by agencies of secondary socialisation.

Young people spend a great deal of time at school, therefore it is very influential.

The media is a very powerful agency of socialisation – especially in terms of body image, violence and gender roles.

Not all children are in families where they are raised in a gender-stereotypical way.

Is primary socialisation an effective form of socialisation?

Refer to the work by Ann Oakley and Fiona Norman mentioned in this chapter.

Children will imitate their parents as they act as role models.

The family is where children first internalise their society's norms, values and culture.

How does primary socialisation have an impact on gender socialisation?

Some sociologists believe that this argument is over simplifying the situation and could be viewed as too deterministic.

Not all children accept the gender stereotypes they are socialised with.

Many children are brought up in feminist households and are subsequently not raised in a gender stereotypical way.

REVISION BOOSTER

Ann Oakley believes that the family is the main agency of gender socialisation. She believes that the family is the institution where children learn the norms and values associated with their gender. She identified, through her research, four main ways in which children learn their gender roles and the norms and values associated with what society believes is masculine and feminine and the cultural differences between them. These four ways are manipulation, canalisation, verbal appellation and boys and girls undertaking different activities and tasks within the home. Fiona Norman further supports the idea that gender stereotypes are learnt and reinforced at home. She says that boys and girls are given gender specific toys to play with, they wear different clothes and take part in different activities.

Think link

Try to think of ways of bringing in what you have learnt about informal social control, cultural diversity and sanctions and how they are linked to primary socialisation.

Knowledge check

1. Describe what is meant by primary socialisation.

   (2 marks)

2. Explain why socialisation by the family is important.

   (4 marks)

Spec spotlight

1.3 The process of socialisation: agents of socialisation

Link to textbook

pp 16–17: Socialisation

pp 18–19: Secondary agents of socialisation

AO2 Apply

Watch some children's television programmes that are popular today. How are these programmes teaching children norms, values and gender roles? Are there any stereotypes being reinforced while the children are watching these?

Children's films can reinforce gender stereotypes. Compare the body shapes and type of Mr and Mrs Incredible in this popular Disney films.

Take it further

Work is an agency of secondary socialisation. When you go to work you go through a process of resocialisation. This resocialisation happens in several ways in terms of rules, norms, dress codes, etc. How and why does this resocialisation take place?

What are agencies of socialisation?

The agencies of socialisation are the people or groups that play a part in the process of socialisation and help to teach us norms and values, for example, education, work, media, peers and religion.

What is secondary socialisation?

Secondary socialisation is when we learn expected behaviour, norms, values and our culture from social networks and agencies of socialisation outside the family. It occurs in later childhood and adulthood. Secondary socialisation overlaps and builds on primary socialisation. Secondary socialisation is a lifelong process and takes place outside the home. It is where children and adults learn how to behave and act in the situations in which they find themselves, for example, at school and in the workplace.

What is informal and formal socialisation?

Informal socialisation is what a person learns about their culture, norms and values, behaviour, etc. as they go about their daily life. Informal socialisation happens by chance. Formal socialisation is when people or organisations deliberately set out to change how others behave.

The workplace is an agency of secondary socialisation.

How powerful is the media as an agency of secondary socialisation?

The media is an important agent of socialisation:

Advertising is very powerful in influencing social attitudes towards gender, social class, age, etc.

Some argue that the media has a direct influence on those who watch it, especially in terms of norms associated with violence.

Susie Orbach and Naomi Wolf believe that the media can influence our idea of the norms associated with female body image due to the representations of how young women are portrayed. They believe that these representations can lead to eating disorders.

Adverts such as 'Mums go to Iceland' and women promoting products such as washing-up liquid can reinforce social norms regarding gender roles.

The horror film *Childs Play 3* is said to have led two ten-year-old boys to murder Jamie Bulger, a toddler in Liverpool, Merseyside.

The media tends to present stereotypical representations of ethnic minorities, for example, tabloids will tend to represent ethnic minorities as a threat to society.

People may react differently to media messages:

Jock Young believes that seeing the effects of violence in the media and the pain and suffering it causes victims and their families actually makes people less inclined to become violent themselves.

The hypodermic syringe model fails to take into account other social and psychological factors.

Eating disorders are complex mental illnesses with many contributing psychological and biological causes.

A study in St Helena by Charton *et al* concluded that there was no difference in children's behaviour before and after television was introduced to the colony.

Not everybody who watches violence in the media becomes violent themselves. Cumberbatch believes that there is no link between watching violence in the media and people actually committing violence in real life.

Some sociologists such as Joke Hermes believe that people can reject media messages and therefore influences about gender stereotypes.

Religion is an important agent of socialisation:

Religion provides people with a moral code to follow, for example, the Ten Commandments in Christianity. These are the norms and values that they will follow.

Religions act as agencies of informal social control by reinforcing the norms of good or bad actions. Those who have been righteous will be rewarded in the afterlife; those who have sinned will be punished for eternity.

Religion can reinforce social class and people's position in society as they may believe that this position has been ordained by God. The Christian hymn 'All things bright and beautiful' supports this with the words 'The rich man in his castle, the poor man at his gate, God made them high and lowly, and ordered their estate.'

Religion may have less influence as an agent of socialisation:

Functionalists like Parsons ignore the negative side of religion where it can cause conflict and divisive societies.

Church attendance and membership has decreased by over 1 million in the last 20 years and the number of couples marrying in a church has decreased.

The impact of secularisation has affected society's views on matters such as divorce and cohabitation.

Knowledge check

1. Describe what is meant by canalisation. **(2 marks)**
2. Identify two agencies of secondary socialisation. **(2 marks)**

Spec spotlight

1.2 Debates over the acquisition of identity: nature/nurture

Link to textbook

pp 14–15: The 'nature versus nurture' debate

pp 20–21: Feral children and the lack of socialisation

AO2 Apply

Research some of the case studies in the table. Which category of feral child would they fit into? Can you summarise their stories in a few sentences, describing how they were raised and what happened to them once they were found? Explain how they can be used in a debate on nature versus nurture and also to explain the importance of primary socialisation.

What is a feral child?

A feral child is a child who may have been neglected by their family, may have been raised by animals and/or have been brought up in isolation without human contact. Cases of feral children can be divided into three types – isolated children, confined children and children raised by animals.

Which case studies can I use in my answers?

Name	Country	Why are they regarded as feral?
Genie Wiley	USA	Severe neglect
Oxana Malaya	Ukraine	Raised by dogs
John Ssebunya	Uganda	Raised by monkeys in the jungle
Danielle Lierow	USA	Severe neglect
Edik	Ukraine	Raised by dogs
Kamala and Amala	India	Lived in the forest

Kamala and Amala, after living with wolves, used to sleep on the ground.

Name	Country	Why are they regarded as feral?
Shamdeo	India	Lived in the forest and raised by wolves
Vanya Yudin	Russia	Treated like a bird by his mother
Marina Chapman	Colombia	Raised by monkeys
Isabelle	USA	Kept in a dark room by her mother
Maria Isabel Quaresma Dos Santos	Portugal	Brought up with chickens

Why might feral children find it difficult to fit into society?

- May not be able to talk so unable to communicate with other people.
- May not walk like other humans.
- May find other humans frightening and so may not want to mix with people.
- Have not been taught the norms and values of society.
- May not eat like other people in their society.

Take it further

John Ssebunya was found aged six years living in the jungle in Uganda. He had fled from home after watching his father murder his mother and was worried that he would be next. The monkeys in the jungle gave him food and he claims they taught him to climb trees and find his own food. When he was found, he was placed in an orphanage and taken care of. Find out what happened after he was rescued and explain how John's story can be used in the nature versus nurture debate.

Cases of feral children support the nurture theory:

Feral children crawl on all fours, eat raw meat and have no language skills.

Although Genie learnt words she was never able to construct a sentence with them.

Oxana, although rescued, still barks and growls like the dogs she was raised with.

Key figure

Oxana Malaya was found as an eight-year-old feral child living in Ukraine in 1991, having lived most of her life in the company of dogs in a dog kennel because her alcoholic parents ignored her. She picked up a number of dog-like habits such as growling, barking and smelling food. She found it difficult to understand and learn language. They lived in a very poor area where there were wild dogs roaming the streets who cared for her. She learnt their behaviours and mannerisms and is said to still find human contact difficult. Oxana Malaya is evidence of nurture theory because she was not socialised by humans and acted like a dog.

Do all cases of feral children support the nurture theory?

Think link

When writing about feral children, try to think of ways of bringing in what you have learnt about nature versus nurture and primary socialisation and how they are linked.

REVISION BOOSTER

Danielle Lierow was rescued at seven years old from her mother who had severely neglected her. She had been kept in a small dark place on her own. She didn't know how to play, walk or talk. She had never been to a doctor or to school. She was unable to eat properly as she had only been fed by a bottle and so could not eat solid food. The officer who found her said it 'was the worst case of child neglect I have seen in 27 years'. Danielle was later adopted into a family where she has learnt some basic life skills but still does not talk. Danielle is a good example to use when writing about the importance of primary socialisation.

Knowledge check

1. Describe what is meant by a feral child. **(2 marks)**

2. Explain why some children are feral. **(2 marks)**

3. Explain two reasons why feral children may have difficulty fitting into society. **(4 marks)**

4. Explain how the study of feral children helps us to understand nurture theory. **(4 marks)**

Spec spotlight

1.3 The process of socialisation: how agents of socialisation pass on culture and identity, for example gender

Link to textbook

pp 16–17: Socialisation
pp 18–19: Secondary agents of socialisation

AO2 Apply

Cumberbatch found that in adverts, women are twice as likely to engage in household activities and men are twice as likely to be represented in paid employment. Look out for how men and women are portrayed in the adverts that you see this week. Is there a difference in how men and women are portrayed?

Take it further

There is a national campaign called 'Let toys be toys' which is about pressuring the toy industry to stop categorising children's toys by gender. It has been very successful with some big high street brands removing 'boys' and 'girls' signage from their shops. Find out why they believe that this is such an important topic and what they have done in order to achieve these successes. How could you use examples from this campaign to support answers about both primary and secondary socialisation?

What is gender identity?

Gender identity is how we think of ourselves and how others think of us in terms of our gender.

What is gender socialisation?

Gender socialisation is when children learn to act as society thinks is appropriate for their sex. For example girls may be given dolls or prams to play with. It is an on-going process that takes place within a family and through other agents of socialisation and continues throughout life.

Primary socialisation: How are gender roles socially constructed and controlled?

Role models/imitation – boys may copy their father doing DIY as this is seen as a masculine thing to do in our society.	Language used – telling children that boys don't cry or calling a girl an angel.	Clothes – pink for girls and blue for boys.
Manipulation – reward a boy for being good at football or dressing a girl in 'pretty' clothes. Parents encourage children to behave in what they perceive to be a gender appropriate way.	Positive sanctions – rewarded for acting in a gender appropriate way.	Negative sanctions – punished for not acting in a gender appropriate way.
Canalisation – direct a girl into doing ballet or playing with dolls and prams as they are associated with femininity.	Parents give children toys and books that are considered the norm for that gender.	Verbal appellations – 'good girl' or 'naughty boy' for example.

Rules, curfews, etc.

What do little girls learn about the norms and values associated with their gender when they are encouraged to dress up as faries or princesses?

Secondary socialisation: How are gender roles socially constructed and controlled?

Agency of secondary socialisation	How people are socialised into their gender roles	
School	• Uniforms – in some schools only boys can wear trousers • Subject choices – boys more likely to study science subjects and girls English and the arts • Gendered regimes – girls play netball, boys play rugby	• Teaching has become feminised – women are more likely to be classroom teachers which gives girls positive role models • Labelling theory • Careers advice
Peer group	• Peer pressure to conform to social norms regarding gender, for example, the clothing worn • Need to fit in and imitation	• Informal sanctions and rewards for not following/following gender roles within the peer group
Mass media	• Imitating stereotypically gender roles, for example, females wishing to look 'sexy' and have a slim figure and males desiring to have a muscular body • Stereotyping portrayals, for example, 'Mum's gone to Iceland'	• Role modelling – for example, females in Hollywood films are often presented as weak, in need of rescuing by a strong male hero • Children's TV programmes/websites/interactive games
Workplace	• Sanctions and rewards • Types of jobs may socialise people into gender roles, for example, a female may be expected to work in childcare and a male may be expected to work in mechanics	• Income, full-/part-time work and glass ceiling
Religion	• Norms, values and beliefs • Key holy figures • Dress codes	• Expectations of behaviour and moral codes

Margaret Mead's research into gender roles:

It was a primary study and through her research she found that the tribes in New Guinea had different ideas about gender than Westerners.

The Tchambuli tribe had gender roles which were very much the opposite to what we might be used to – the men were quiet, emotional, sat around gossiping and preening themselves and were seen as delicate whereas the women were bossy and looked after the finances. It showed that gender roles are learnt rather than innate.

Her studies found gender differences between each tribe which suggests that culture influences gender.

Key figure

Margaret Mead was an anthropologist who studied tribes in New Guinea and talked to them about their cultures. Mead could not speak their language which reduces the reliability of the study. Her research was an overt observation – they knew they were being watched and could have altered their behaviour.

Think link

Think about what you have learnt about feminism, education and media and how they are linked to gender socialisation.

Knowledge check

1. Describe what is meant by gender. **(2 marks)**
2. Describe what is meant by gender roles. **(2 marks)**
3. Identify and explain two ways in which children are socialised into gender roles. **(4 marks)**
4. Explain how children may learn gender roles from schools. **(5 marks)**

Spec spotlight

1.3 The process of socialisation: how agents of socialisation pass on culture and identity, for example, class and ethnic identity

Link to textbook
pp 28–29: Class, ethnic and national identity

AO2 Apply

Ofsted now judges schools on how they teach their students 'British Values'. Find out what these British Values consist of. How are they taught in your school? Are these values taught discreetly or as part of the hidden curriculum?

OFSTED now judges schools on how well they teach 'British Values.'

Take it further

Richard Weight believes that the English football team binds the English nation together. He sees national identity as being about emotional and cultural achievements.

What is identity?

Identity is how we see ourselves and how others see us. It is formed by our family, our life experiences and the people with whom we come into contact day to day, whether that is at home, school or work.

	Class Identity	Ethnic Identity	National Identity
Family	Use of restricted and elaborated code.	Food eaten at home, religion followed, clothes worn, for example, wearing a headscarf.	Language spoken at home, festivals celebrated, films watched together, for example, Bollywood.
School	Through setting and streaming, labelling and teacher expectations.	They may teach the language of the country. For example, children in Wales are taught Welsh at school.	Through assemblies, school holidays for national festivals and through meeting Ofsted's focus on teaching British Values.
Media	Reinforced through soap operas, documentaries and the news.	Some ethnic minorities may be portrayed negatively.	Will show national sporting events on TV. Important occasions such as Remembrance Day are televised.

Does the England football team bring us together as one nation?

There may be several national identities in Britain:

We live in a multicultural society with many different symbols and ethnicities.

Time and age can make a difference to the definition of a UK national identity – what it means to be British today is different to a teenager and to a pensioner.

There are many regional differences and identities within the UK. For example, Liverpool has a very different accent to Surrey, has a regional dish 'Scouse' and traditional songs such as 'In my Liverpool Home'.

Is it difficult to describe a national identity in the UK?

Many people in the UK support the national football teams passionately.

Michael Schudson believes that being English is seen as central to our cultural identity.

The UK has a number of national traditions and rituals, for example, Remembrance Sunday in November.

Do we learn part of our national identity through an ethnocentric curriculum?

Key figure

Michael Schudson says that we are socialised into our national identity and culture through the media and education. For example, the curriculum at school is ethnocentric and we learn the music, literature and art of our nation. The media socialises us into our national identity by showing national events such as royal weddings, royal funerals and Remembrance Day services in November. Schudson also believes that symbols such as coins and flags socialise us into our national identity.

Think link
Remember what you have learnt about primary and secondary socialisation and the hidden curriculum and how they are linked to identity.

Take it further

Some people may have a dual national identity which can create conflict within a person with regards to their culture and how they see themselves. Orin Begum is a corporate lawyer and a poet who was born in Bangladesh but was brought up and lives in the East End of London. She has written a poem about her experiences of living within two very different cultures. Find a copy of her poem, Brown Girl, and read it through. Think about the difficulties our national identity/identities can create.

Knowledge check

1. Explain what is meant by identity. **(2 marks)**

2. Describe how schools can encourage a feeling of national identity. **(4 marks)**

3. Describe the difference between race and ethnicity. **(4 marks)**

4. Describe how the family can help to create an individual's identity. **(5 marks)**

Spec spotlight

1.3 The process of socialisation: formal and informal social control

Link to textbook
pp 30–31: Social control

AO2 Apply

Think about a typical day in your life – what sanctions both positive and negative have you received? Which agencies of socialisation gave you those sanctions? Which were formal and which were informal? Which were the most and least effective and why?

Take it further

The prison system and young offenders institutions are formal agents of social control. There is an organisation called 'End Child Imprisonment' which is campaigning to close all children's prisons and young offenders institutes. Find out why some people believe that prisons for children are not an effective form of social control in the UK today.

The police are a formal agent of social control.

What is social control?

Social control describes the different ways in which society tries to make sure that its members conform to laws, rules and norms.

What is informal social control?

Informal social control is based on unwritten rules which people are expected to follow. They are enforced by social pressure which can be very powerful.

Informal agent of social control	How agent controls members
Family	Through sanctions such as grounding or 'telling off'. Younger children may have time out on the 'naughty step'.
Friends	Friendship groups may leave other members out of activities or from the group itself.
Local community	Disapproval of others in local community.
School	Disapproval of teachers, criticism, and peer group pressure. Detentions, warnings or being placed in isolation.

Being excluded from a peer group is a form of informal social control.

What is formal social control?

Formal social control is based on written rules and laws. These rules are written down by the agencies of socialisation and the sanctions are clearly stated. Agencies of formal social control have a lot of power and can make people conform as they can often lead to serious and negative consequences.

Formal agent of social control	How agent controls society
Police	They enforce the law, keep order in society and investigate crime.
Government	They make laws which govern and regulate our behaviour.
Courts	Courts decide what sanctions lawbreakers will receive.
Prisons and other sanctions	They punish law breakers and deter others from committing crimes.

Formal agents of social control can be powerful:

They have a lot of power and control in society and can lead to very serious negative consequences which people are fearful of.

The government make and implement the laws that people have to follow.

The courts implement the law and can sentence people to prison.

Does prison work?

Informal agents of social control can be powerful:

People can go against the agencies of formal social control – for example, the Croydon riots.

If other agencies of formal social control were effective, then there would be no need for the prison system.

The family has a closer relationship with people and is more flexible therefore is more effective.

Women in prison

Prison is a form of social control but the question is often asked 'does prison work?' Women in Prison is a national charity which believes that the criminal justice system in the UK is failing women. It found that women are more likely to re-offend than men who have similar sentences and they are twice as likely as men to require mental health help in prison. Women in Prison believes that women who are not a risk to society should not be imprisoned. In 2017, 84 per cent of women in prison had committed non-violent offences, such as theft and handling stolen goods, and 26 per cent had no previous convictions. Research by this charity found that 48 per cent of women are re-convicted within one year of leaving prison. Is prison an effective form of social control or is there a more suitable alternative?

Think link
Think about what you have learnt about crime and deviance and how they are linked to social control.

Knowledge check
1. Describe what is meant by social control. **(2 marks)**
2. Identify two agencies of social control. **(2 marks)**

Spec spotlight

2.1 Family diversity and different family forms in the UK and within a global context: what is a family? types of family, global family forms, one-child policy in China

Link to textbook

pp 34–35: What is a family?

pp 36–37: Global families

pp 38–39: Different types of family in Britain today

AO2 Apply

What were the reasons for China introducing the one-child policy in 1979? What social and ethical problems did the one-child policy create in Chinese society? Why might Chinese couples be reluctant to have more than one child today?

Take it further

What concerns might the Chinese government have about the country having a low birth rate and an ageing population?

Functionalists regard the nuclear family as the ideal family type.

Families and households

There were 27.2 million households in the UK in 2017.	The number of households has increased by 6 per cent since 2007, similar to the growth in the UK population during this period.
Families and households are not considered to be the same.	A family is a group of people related by blood or marriage. A household is a group of people who live together but are not related by blood or marriage.
There are many different types of family.	A family is a married, civil partnered or cohabiting couple with or without children, or a lone parent, with at least one child, who live at the same address. Children may be dependent or non-dependent. Reconstituted or blended families can involve a couple with children from previous relationships as well as the couple's own children.
Households can also exist in different forms.	A household is one person living alone, or a group of people (not necessarily related) living at the same address who share cooking facilities and share a living room, sitting room or dining area. According to a recent ONS survey, a household can consist of a single family, more than one family or no families in the case of a group of unrelated people.
The most common type of family in the UK is the nuclear family.	This is made of a male and female parent and their children, either biological or adopted. It is the preferred choice of many politicians and the media.

Families around the world

Polygamy refers to any marriage in which one partner has several legal partners at the same time.	The most common form is for one man to have several wives, although the opposite (polyandry) does exist. It is often found in traditional societies, and even there is often only practised by the rich.
Arranged marriages involve parents choosing their children's spouses for them.	These are often done between two families of similar status and are more to do with strengthening family alliances than with love.
In 1979 China began to restrict family size due to the size of the population.	China has been slowly getting rid of its one-child policy over the last five years due to its ageing population and low birth rate. Now all couples in China are allowed to have two children if they wish.

Strengths of the functionalist definition of the family are:		
Functionalists such as G. P. Murdock and Talcott Parsons and New Right sociologists believe the nuclear family is the ideal and the one that works the best.	Murdock gives four functions of the nuclear family – sexual, reproduction, economic and socialisation.	Parsons gives two functions – primary socialisation and stabilisation of adult personalities.
The sexual function means people's sex drive gets stable satisfaction best in a monogamous relationship and this also contributes to creating a new generation of children through reproduction.	The economic need for food and shelter is most efficiently met in a nuclear family.	Socialisation in the nuclear family helps teach basic norms and values.

Weaknesses of the functionalist definition of the family are:		
Functionalists have been criticised for idealising the family.	Murdock makes no reference to alternative households to the family or to disharmony and problems in family relationships.	Murdock's idea of the family is ethnocentric and is based on the notion that the Western culture is the ideal.
Feminists argue that the nuclear family is too patriarchal and repressive.	They do not look at issues of conflict, class and violence in relation to the family. These occur in all families including the nuclear.	They do not take into account legal changes such as same-sex marriages and allowing unmarried couples to adopt.

Knowledge check

1. Describe what is meant by a 'reconstituted family'.
   (2 marks)
2. Outline the functionalist view on the nuclear family.
   (4 marks)
3. Explain what sociologists mean by family diversity.
   (4 marks)
4. Explain why there has been an increase in civil partnerships.
   (4 marks)

Think link

Although this revision spread is about the different types of family, try to also think of ways of bringing in different sociological perspectives and how they are linked.

Key figure

G.P. Murdock was a functionalist who studied 250 societies. He believed that family is universal and the nuclear family is the ideal type. He identified four functions of the nuclear family – sexual, reproductive, socialisation and economic.

There are many different types of family in the UK today.

Spec spotlight

2.2 Social changes and family structures: divorce rates and serial monogamy, cohabitation, lone-parent families, later age of marriage, singlehood

Link to textbook

pp 40–41: Changing marriage patterns
pp 48–49: The growth in singlehood

AO2 Apply

Sue Sharpe found that the majority of 11–16 year olds regard marriage as 'a choice rather than a necessity'. Do you agree with this statement? Why? Make a list of the reasons why marriage might no longer be viewed as a necessity. Ask your friends and family for their opinion on Sue Sharpe's finding. Do they agree with her? Is there a generational difference in your answers? Why might this be?

Take it further

Does the mass media have an influence over people's attitudes towards marriage? Think about the soap operas, films and box sets that are on television today– what examples of families, relationships and marriages can you see? Is marriage the norm? Speak to your parents and grandparents – do they think that the relationships and families in the media have changed since they were children and teenagers? Can they give you any examples?

Marriage in decline

Marriage has declined over the last 50 years.	In 2001 the lowest number of marriages took place in the UK since records began. Over the same period, there has been an increase in the number of adults cohabiting.
Anthony Giddens says people are more likely to have a series of cohabitations rather than a lifelong marriage.	This is known as serial monogamy. Cohabitation is seen as a long-term alternative to marriage. Giddens supports this by saying this is because people expect more from relationships and are less likely to accept being in an 'empty' marriage.
Other social changes have contributed to the decline in marriage.	The impact of feminism may have made marriage less attractive. Additionally, as seen in the media, the fear of divorce may convince people to not get married in the first place.
Marriage is now seen as a choice.	Secularisation (only 8 per cent of people go to church on a regular basis) means the religious aspect of marriage is less important. Also contributing to this change in view of marriage are the change in gender roles (women prioritising careers), social attitudes (marriage seen as unimportant) and the cost of weddings (average being £20–£25k). The cost of housing may now be now a priority over marriage, if the choice is between a wedding or house deposit.

Modern marriages

However, in 2011, 65 per cent of couples were still married.	Marriage is still seen as an important event in someone's life, as shown by the amount of money people are willing to spend on a wedding.
New forms of families use marriage even as it declines in nuclear families.	Reconstituted families are still married. The Marriage Act (2013) means that same sex-couples can now also marry.
Some see the decline as people delaying marriage rather than not getting married at all.	The average age of marriage has been steadily increasing. Most people do get married at some point in their life, cohabitation may be just a prelude rather than an alternative to marriage, almost like a trial run. Also, it is important to note that most households are still led by a married couple.
Social changes mean some benefits of marriage can now be achieved outside of marriage.	There has been an increase in births outside of marriage which is now more socially acceptable (50 per cent of births registered have parents that are not married). Siobhan McLaughlin won a court battle over benefits for widows which demonstrated that cohabiting couples are equal to married couples.

Other differences

There are still differences between the status of cohabitees and married couples. For instance, if one partner in a cohabiting relationship dies without a will, the surviving partner will not automatically inherit anything.

Not all couples choose to get married. Why might they make this decision?

Positive outcomes of the possible decline of marriage are:

Feminists see the decline of marriage as positive as marriage is a patriarchal institute.

They also believe the decline in marriage reflects the increase in women's rights and opportunities.

It may reflect the reality of women being able to go further in their careers.

Marxists believe that marriage is a consumerist choice.

It may show that people value emotional needs more and as such are less likely to marry.

Negative outcomes of the possible decline of marriage are:

Functionalists say the decline in marriage means less effective primary socialisation, which is not positive.

They also think it means a decline in morality, which means more problem children.

Functionalists believe the decline in family has had a negative effect on society.

In 2015, 56 per cent of same-sex marriages were between female couples

REVISION BOOSTER

A survey by the ONS shows that marriages between men and women in the UK fell to a record low in 2015. Men and women under the age of 20 have seen the biggest decrease whereas, in contrast, the number of men aged 50 and above has actually increased. The rising cost of weddings is given as one of the reasons for the decline of marriage, with some research suggesting that the average wedding will cost over £32,000 by 2028.

Think link

When you think about the decline of marriage, try to also think of ways of bringing in changes in the divorce rate, cohabitation, singlehood and lone-parent families.

Key figure

The **Great British Class Survey** believes that people will only wish to marry if they can find a partner who provides them with personal fulfilment. The need for intimacy, closeness and emotional satisfaction has been recognised as more important than social norms of marriage.

Knowledge check

1. Describe what is meant by cohabitation. (2 marks)

2. Identify two ways that secularisation may have led to a decline in marriage in Britain today. (4 marks)

3. Explain the decline in marriage in Britain today. You should explore at least two reasons in your response. (8 marks)

4. 'The family is in crisis.' Do you agree with this view? (15 marks)

AO2 Apply

Research Peter Wilmott's study of North London and his idea of three types of extended family. What are the names of these types of family and how are they described? Can you recognise your family in any of these descriptions?

Take it further

Think about films and programmes you watch – which of Wilmott's types of extended family can you recognise?

There are around 2 million single parents in Britain today.

Family diversity

Family diversity refers to the different types of family in Britain today.

Rhona and Robert Rapoport state that diversity is at the heart of family life. They say we live in a pluralistic society. The different types of family include nuclear, lone-parent, childless reconstituted, extended, beanpole, civil partnership and cohabitation.

Not all types of family are equally common.

With 12.9 million families, the married or civil partner couple family remains the most common in 2017, with the cohabiting couple family growing the fastest, according to the ONS.

Civil partnerships and same-sex families are becoming increasingly common.

Reasons for this include legal changes, secularisation, changing social attitudes, the media, the gay rights movement and the ability for homosexual couples to have children through IVF, adoption or surrogacy.

Opposite-sex couples are more likely to be married than same-sex couples.

The most likely reason for this is because of the relatively recent introduction of civil partnerships and marriages for same-sex couples.

Family type	Thousands		
	2017		
	With dependent children	Without dependent children[2]	Total families
Married couple family[1]	4,944	7,890	12,834
Opposite sex married couple family	4,938	7,862	12,800
Same sex married couple family	6	28	34
Civil partner couple family[3]	8	47	55
Cohabiting couple family[1]	1,251	2,040	3,291
Opposite sex cohabiting couple family	1,246	1,943	3,190
Same sex cohabiting couple family	4	97	101
Lone parent family	1,781	1,037	2,817
All families	7,983	11,014	18,997

Notes:
1. Married couple and cohabiting couple families include both opposite sex and same sex married couples.
2. Families without dependent children have only non-dependent children or no children in the household.
3. Civil partnerships were introduced in the UK in December 2005.
4. Marriages to same sex couples were introduced in England and Wales in March 2014.

Detailed family types, UK, 2017 (Source: Labour Force Survey, Office for National Statistics)

Reasons for family diversity

There have been many changes in norms and values.

Changing patterns of marriage, divorce and cohabitation have affected family diversity.

Other trends such as increasing secularisation have also had an impact.

Religion is no longer as important today and does not have the same influence on people.

The changing position of women has increased family diversity.

There have been legal changes such as the Equal Pay Act as well as women's careers being more important.

Economic factors have contributed.

The Equal Pay Act also contributes to women being more economically independent. The welfare system means lone parents do not have to marry for economic reasons.

Strengths of the Rapoports view of family diversity are:

They believe that there is no 'correct' type of family and Britain is no longer dominated by one family type.	They believe that the changes in the types of family are positive as it gives people more choices in their lives.	They take into account differences in class and culture and the age of the people in the family.

Weaknesses of the Rapoports view of family diversity are:

The Rapoports say that families are households but households are not necessarily families.	Doesn't take into account the increase of single person households.	They used secondary sources, secondary data and the work of other sociologists.

Strengths of Robert Chester's view of family diversity are:

Robert Chester acknowledges that that there has some been an increase in family diversity and doesn't see this as negative.	He believes that the extent of family diversity has been exaggerated and that the nuclear family is still the dominant family type but one where both the male and the female play an equally important role (neo-conventional family). Somerville supports his view.	He argues that the while the statistics are showing a decline in the traditional nuclear family, they are not taking into account the ageing population and the inevitable increase of widows and widowers no longer living in nuclear families.

Weaknesses of Robert Chester's view of family diversity are:

The number of people living in nuclear families is declining.	Boulton found that while men may help out more with the childcare it is still women who are the primary caregivers.	The British Social Attitudes Survey found that women still do the majority of the housework.

REVISION BOOSTER

Although this revision spread is about family diversity try to also think of ways of bringing in the different types of family and the various sociological perspectives on the family and how they are linked.

Key figure

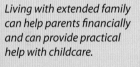

Robert Chester is a sociologist who argues that the nuclear family is still the main family type. He says this is shown in the majority of people getting married and no divorcing, in cohabitation still often being a trial run for marriage, that most people have experience of a nuclear family and that divorced people often remarry.

Living with extended family can help parents financially and can provide practical help with childcare.

Knowledge check

1. Describe what is meant by family diversity. **(2 marks)**

2. Outline two ways in which family life may vary between ethnic groups. **(4 marks)**

3. Explain the increase in lone-parent families in Britain today. You should explore at least two reasons in your response. **(8 marks)**

4. Evaluate the view that changing norms and values have contributed to growing diversity in family life today. **(15 marks)**

AO2 Apply

Write a sentence for each of the reasons for the increase in lone-parent families, explaining why each factor could lead to an increase in lone-parent families.

Take it further

J. K. Rowling, author of *Harry Potter*, said 'I am prouder of my years as a single mother than of any other part of my life'. What barriers might J. K. Rowling have had to face and overcome in society as a single parent?

There are around 2 million lone-parent families in Britain today.

Functionalists believe that the nuclear family is the best type of family or society. Murdock is a functionalist who sums up their view of the family when he says "No society has succeeded in finding an adequate substitute for the nuclear family…"

Lone-parent families

A lone parent is a parent who cares for a child or children without the assistance of another parent in the home.	This could be due to divorce or family breakdown, death of one parent or a conscious choice by a parent to raise their child on their own.
There are around 2 million lone-parent families – they make up nearly 25 per cent of families with dependent children.	In 1971 this figure was 8 per cent. UK households containing one lone-parent family increased from 2.3 million in 1996 to 2.7 million in 2017. Some figures suggest the number of lone-parent families has tripled since 1971. The UK has one of the highest percentage of lone-parent families in Europe.
However, statistics can't just be taken at face value.	Children may start their life in a lone-parent family, but the single parent may find a new partner, so that the children then live with two parents. The lone-parent charity Gingerbread claims that, on average, single parenthood lasts around five years.
There is a link between poverty and lone-parent families.	47 per cent of children in lone-parent families live in relative poverty, around twice the risk of relative poverty faced by children in couple families (24 per cent).

Why has there been an increase in lone-parent families?

Divorce is more common, which in turn leads to more lone-parent families.	Changes such as higher expectations of marriage and legal changes have contributed to an increase in the divorce rate.
There has been a change in the norms and values regarding single parents.	There is less stigma involved in being a lone-parent family. Trends such as secularisation mean people are no longer as influenced by religion or believe children should only be born within marriage.
There are other ways to have children without being married or cohabiting.	The UK has high rates of teenage pregnancy. Medical changes such as IVF have allowed women to have babies without a partner and women are not afraid of the consequences.
Economic changes have made a difference to single parents.	The Equal Pay Act and the welfare state have contributed to this.

Functionalists believe lone-parent families are 'problems'? Is this true?		
Lone-parent families cannot provide proper socialisation or role models.	New Right sociologist Charles Murray blames the generosity of the welfare state.	Murray believes that lone-parent families without a father as the head of the household are responsible for the increase in the crime rate for young males.

Functionalists believe lone-parent families are 'problems'? Is this false?		
Home Office statistics suggest there is no difference between the crime rates of children from lone-parent families and children from two-parent families.	Other institutions within society could also perform the functions of the family and therefore the lone-parent family is not at a disadvantage.	Cutting benefits will lead to an increase in poverty and further social problems and increase in crime.

Feminists believe lone-parent families are 'problems'? Is this true?		
Lone-parent families give women freedom and independence.	The welfare state allows women to escape from domestic abuse.	Jesse Bernard suggested that marriage was twice as good for men as it is for women.

Feminists believe lone-parent families are 'problems'? Is this false?		
Faust and McKibben say divorced families are seen as deviant and a threat to social order.	When there is no male role model in a family this can be negative.	Feminism ignores the positive side of the family.

Over 80 per cent of lone-parent families are headed by females.

Think link

Think of ways of bringing in what you have learned about divorce and the decline of marriage and how they are linked when you write about lone-parent families.

Key figures

Allan and Crow believe that the number of lone-parent families is due to an increase in marital breakdown and a rise in births to unmarried mothers. They say that this is due to a change in attitudes and society being more accepting of the different types of family today.

Knowledge check

1. Describe what is meant by a lone-parent family. **(2 marks)**

2. Explain two reasons why there has been an increase in lone-parent families.

(8 marks)

AO2 Apply

Have a look at the list of what costs more as a single person rather than a couple (page 31, under the heading 'Is the growth of singlehood negative?', right-hand column). Write a sentence for each one to explain why they cost more. What other items or purchases do you think cost more as a single person?

In 2016, around 7.7 million people lived alone in the UK.

Take it further

The growth in singlehood has created a number of problems for society – it has pushed up the demand for housing, and it is costly in terms of state benefits and the NHS and social services. Research and explain why singlehood is costly in terms of these factors.

Single person households

Single person households are becoming more common in the UK.	29 per cent of UK households are single person households. Single person households may result from divorce, death or a relationship breaking down or they may be a deliberate choice.
In 2017, there were 3.9 million people living alone aged 16 to 64 years.	A larger proportion were male (58.5 per cent). Similarly there were 3.8 million people living alone aged 65 and over but a larger proportion (66.5 per cent) was female.

Why are more people living alone?

The decline in marriage has contributed to this.	People are getting married later in life so live on their own for longer. People choose to live alone before marriage or cohabitation. There has also been a rise in divorce, with one parent living alone.
There have been changes in social attitudes towards singlehood.	There is less stigma attached to remaining single.
Longer life expectancy has had an impact (around half of single person households are age 60+).	This is especially true for females – women are outliving their spouses by decades, rather than years. The changing role of women means women can now afford to live on their own with financial independence.

Changes in employment and travel have had an effect.	People may have to live alone due to increased geographical mobility and changing employment patterns. With an increase in international migrants, for example, students who move to the UK from other countries, there are more people who would not live with their families.
Increase in availability of contraception.	Women can live as a single-person family rather than becoming a lone-parent family (or other family).

Is the growth of singlehood positive?

People are more able to afford to live alone.

In young people, this is only a phase before cohabitation, marriage and/or beginning a nuclear family.

There is a difference between being lonely and alone – divorced or separated people will say that it is lonely to live with the wrong person.

The communications revolution has allowed people to have the benefits of a social life even when they are living alone.

Alone but not lonely.

Is the growth of singlehood negative?

It has increased the demand for housing.

People who live alone are more likely to need the NHS or social services. It is expensive in terms of the welfare state.

According to a Good Housekeeping Institute Study, single life can cost people up to £2000 more a year. Holidays, insurance, gym memberships, council tax, train fares, flights and even wills can cost more as a single person.

All household bills cost proportionally more as a single person.

Spec spotlight

2.2 Social changes and family structures: divorce rates

Link to textbook
pp 50–51: Changes in the divorce rate
pp 52–52: Sociological views on divorce

Divorce changes

Nearly one in two marriages ends in divorce.	According to the ONS, an estimated 43 per cent of marriages end in divorce. There were 13 divorces an hour in England and Wales in 2012.
Divorces can happen for a variety of reasons, and at a variety of points in a marriage.	Almost half of divorces occur in the first ten years of marriage. Women are granted 65 per cent of all divorces. One in seven divorces is granted as a result of adultery.
The average age of divorce is 45 for men and 42 for women.	In 2012, 67 per cent of divorces in the UK were for first marriages. 9 per cent of couples divorcing have both been divorced before. 48 per cent of couples divorcing had at least one child aged under 16 living in the family.
There are legal reasons for the increase in divorce.	In 1969, the Divorce Reform Act introduced the concept of irretrievable breakdown of marriage. The 1984 Matrimonial Proceedings Act meant people could get a divorce after one year.

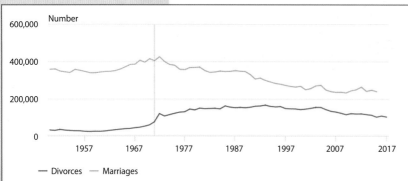

Number of marriages and divorces of opposite-sex couples, 1950 to 2017. (Source: Office for National Statistics)

Divorce is easier and cheaper to get and men and women both have the right to file for divorce.

The introduction of legal aid to help those on low incomes is a legal reason which has made divorce easier and cheaper. The reasons why a man or woman may legally divorce have changed and therefore made divorce easier to obtain.

Financial reasons also have a relationship with the increase in divorce.	The welfare state and making divorce cheaper has had an impact. Women are also less financially dependent on men.

Views on divorce

The increase in divorce can be linked to feminist views and women enjoying more freedoms.	Up to three quarters of divorces are filed by women. There are now more employment opportunities for women. Legal changes such as the Equal Pay Act and Sex Discrimination Act have had an effect.
Secularisation has had a role to play as well.	Religion has less influence over people in society and so people are not influenced by religious vows made in front of God such as 'till death do us part' and 'what God has joined together let not man separate.'
Changing social attitudes to divorce mean people are less fearful of it.	There is less stigma to being divorced; it is more socially acceptable. Royal family and celebrities getting married and divorced sets a standard for society.
Higher expectations from marriages mean people are less likely to put up with a bad marriage.	Again, example in the media, including the royal family, set a standard for what people should expect from a good marriage. In the past people married for economic reasons, now it is more for love and happiness.
Increased life expectancy leads inevitably to an increase in divorce.	Marriages can last longer; there is more time for things to go wrong in a marriage. People no longer feel that they cannot be divorced after a certain age.

AO2 Apply

What are the effects of divorce on husbands and wives, on the children and on the family as a whole?

Strengths of the feminist view of divorce:

Divorce is not negative as it means that women are breaking free from the oppression of the patriarchal nuclear family.

Jesse Bernard claims the rising divorce rate shows that women are becoming more confident about rejecting patriarchy in marriage.

Wendy Sigle-Rushton says working mothers are more likely to divorce than non-working mothers due to factors such as dual burden.

Weaknesses of the feminist view of divorce:

Divorce does not always benefit women – lone-parent families can have a higher chance of experiencing poverty.

Functionalists do not agree that divorce is beneficial as they believe children will not get the same level of primary socialisation.

Cooke and Gash found no evidence to support Sigle-Rushton's view that working-women are more likely to divorce than non-working women.

Strengths of the New Right view of divorce:

Divorce undermines the traditional nuclear family which is essential for society.

Divorce creates an underclass of single parents dependent on the welfare state.

Murray argues that the welfare state rewards having children without having to pay for them. He calls this a 'perverse incentive'.

Weaknesses of the New Right view of divorce:

Functionalists argue that people remarry after divorce and therefore have not rejected marriage as an institution within society.

Lone parents are more likely to be in poverty. Rodgers and Pryor's research further supports this.

Absent parents have to pay child maintenance. The government also provides help to allow single parents to work, in the form of child tax credit for example.

A recent survey by the Department for Work and Pensions found that 90 per cent of single parents did not want to claim benefits and 55 per cent would work if there was adequate day care.

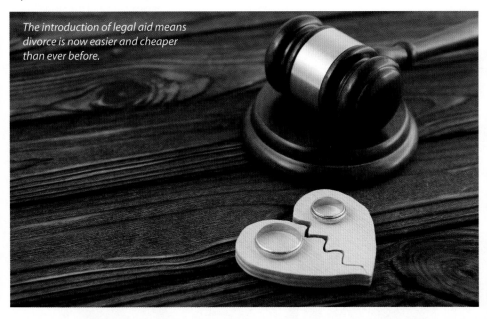

The introduction of legal aid means divorce is now easier and cheaper than ever before.

REVISION BOOSTER

In 2004 the Civil Partnership Act allowed for legal dissolution of civil partnerships for the same reasons as a marriage – the court is satisfied that there is irretrievable breakdown. In 2014 same-sex marriages became law and the same grounds for divorce applied to both same-sex and opposite-sex couples.

There are five specific grounds for divorce: adultery, unreasonable behaviour, desertion, separation for more than two years (if both parties agree) or separation for more than five years even without agreement.

Think link

You could also talk about the effects of divorce on different people and on society as a whole.

Key figure

Talcott Parsons is a functionalist who believes that the increase in divorce has a negative effect. He argued that married couples with a clear division of labour could provide comfort and emotional support, which he compared to having a 'warm bath' that would relax and soothe people from the stresses of modern life.

Knowledge check

1. Describe what is meant by secularisation. **(2 marks)**
2. Outline the feminist view on the reasons for the change in the divorce rate. **(4 marks)**
3. Explain two legal reasons for the increase in the divorce rate. **(4 marks)**
4. Discuss reasons for changes in divorce rates in the UK. **(15 marks)**

Is the family in decline? Is the nuclear family under threat?

Description

Spec spotlight

2.2 Social changes and family structures: cohabitation, lone-parent families, later age of marriage

2.5 Criticisms of family: marital breakdown and divorce, decline of the traditional family

Link to textbook

pp 54–55: Changes to family sizes
pp 56–57: Is 'the family' in decline?

AO2 Apply

Sue Sharpe found that the majority of 11–16 year olds regard marriage as 'a choice rather than a necessity'. Do you agree with this statement? Why? Make a list of the reasons why marriage might no longer be viewed as a necessity.

Take it further

Ask your friends and family for their opinion on Sue Sharpe's findings. Do they agree with her? Is there a generational difference in your answers? Why might this be?

Is the family in decline?

This depends on what you define as a family – a nuclear family or any type of family?	According to official statistics, the number of nuclear families is decreasing therefore marking a decline in the traditional family.	The effect of the gay rights movement, legal changes to same-sex relationships, changes in social attitudes, adoption and technological changes (IVF, surrogacy) mean that the number of homosexual families are increasing. These are a form of family too.
There is a multi-factorial nature of change, so no single change can take place in isolation.	Social stigma, influence of media and secularisation all have an impact.	In 2017, around 28 per cent of households contained one person. The proportion of one-person households has increased considerably since the early 1970s. A household is not a family but a family can make up a household.
Fewer people are getting married.	The cohabiting-couple family is the fastest growing, therefore the family is not in decline.	A family where the parents are not married is still a family.

Is the nuclear family under threat?

More people choose to live alone or as couples without children.	The number of people living in families with children fell from 52 per cent in 1961 to 36 per cent in 2009.	Rapoport and Rapoport say that while the nuclear family is an option there are other options too. They do not see these options as a threat to the nuclear family but as a positive move towards personal choice.
The married or civil partner couple family remains the most common in 2017.	Cohabiting couple families have been more common than lone-parent families in the UK in the last few years. Chester says that the majority of cohabiting couples are planning on marriage and therefore will form a nuclear family.	The ONS says there is 'an increasing trend to cohabit instead of marry, or to cohabit before marriage'.

Families now come in many shapes and forms.

AOS Evaluation

Is the family in decline? Is the nuclear family under threat? 35

Strengths of the view that the nuclear family is under threat are:

There are more divorces now. 43 per cent of marriages end in divorce.	There has been a growth in child-free families accompanied by the increased acceptability of contraception.	There has been an impact of the changing role of men and the increase of women in the workplace and their changing status in society.
There are more cohabiting couples than ever before.	The effect of the gay rights movement and legal changes to same-sex relationships have changed views of families, as well as secularisation.	An ONS survey in 2015 found that the size of the average family had fallen to an all-time low with women having an average of 1.9 children.
The New Right believe that the family is in decline as they believe that it is only the nuclear family which is the 'correct' family type.	Changing norms and values such as views of single parents and teenage parents.	Change in social attitudes have been accompanied by changes in how parents have children, through adoption or technological changes such as IVF or surrogacy.

Weaknesses of the view that the nuclear family is under threat are:

Families that split up can become reconstituted families.	With extended families, changes in technology allow for regular contact and support at a distance.	Increased freedoms for women have been accompanied by the growth of the New Man and house husbands.
Most of those who cohabit marry eventually. Cohabitation is still often a trial marriage.	Homosexual families are a form of family.	Fewer children in a family is still a family.
It can be ethnocentric. The importance of extended family in other communities, such as those in South Asian cultures, can be different.	Lone-parent and teenage-parent families are forms of family.	ONS figures show that in 2017 there were 19 million families in the UK, a 15 per cent increase from 16.6 million in 1996.

REVISION BOOSTER

You can also talk about the differences that ethnic minorities bring to family. African-Caribbean families have a higher proportion of lone-parent households. In 2012 over half of families with dependent children headed by a black person were lone-parent families. Bangladeshi, Pakistani and Indian households tend to have three generations but most are in fact nuclear rather than extended.

Larger Asian households reflect the value placed on extended families in Asian cultures.

Key figure

Brenda Almond believes that the traditional family is fragmenting and breaking down. This is for a number of reasons, for example, not as many people are getting married, the number of divorces is increasing and technological changes such as IVF which leads to children being raised by adults who are not their biological parents. Almond believes this fragmentation of the family is the cause of many of the problems in society today.

Think link

If you are thinking about the decline of the nuclear family, try to also think of ways of bringing in changes in the divorce rate, cohabitation, sociological perspectives on the family and differences between ethnicities and cultures.

Knowledge check

1. Describe what is meant by the nuclear family. **(2 marks)**
2. Identify two reasons for the increased number of lone-parent families today. **(4 marks)**
3. Explain two reasons why the family might be undergoing change today. **(8 marks)**
4. 'The increase in the divorce rate reflects a decline in the traditional nuclear family.' Is this statement accurate?

   (15 marks)

Children can build close relationships with their grandparents when they live in an extended family.

Spec spotlight

2.3 Social changes and family relationships: segregated and joint conjugal roles, symmetrical families, domestic division of labour, New Man

Link to textbook

pp 58–59: Changes in conjugal roles
pp 60–61: How far have conjugal roles changed?
pp 62–63: The changing role of men in society and in the family

AO2 Apply

Research the studies by Young and Wilmott of working class families in the East End of London, by Norman Henriques and Clifford Slaughter of mining families and Jeremy Tunstall of families of deep sea fishermen. What do you learn about conjugal roles from these studies? How could you apply these to a GCSE question about conjugal roles?

Take it further

There have been a number of recent government initiatives designed to help encourage mothers back into employment. These include shared parental leave and improved childcare provision. How do these government initiatives work and are they deemed successful. If not, why is this?

What do Young and Wilmott mean by joint conjugal roles?

Functionalists, such as Talcott Parsons, believe that it is 'natural' that there are segregated conjugal roles within the family such as the women being housewives and taking care of the children and men being the breadwinners. These segregated roles are needed for the family to run properly.

Conjugal roles

There has been a change in conjugal roles over the last fifty years or so.	There has been a shift from segregated to integrated conjugal roles – shared decision making, performing similar domestic tasks, having a number of common interests and activities.
In the 1960s, Hannah Gavron found that within households there seemed to be more shared conjugal roles than in the past.	Michael Young and Peter Wilmott in 1975 talked about the growth of the symmetrical family – the idea that authority and household chores are shared between married or cohabitating partners. This is similar to integrated conjugal roles. Men are now completing more of a share of the household tasks and women are becoming breadwinners. There is some evidence of men becoming more involved in childcare. Men are more home centred.
Young and Wilmott also take a 'March of Progress' view and say that life is improving within the family, with conjugal relationships becoming more equal and democratic.	Jonathan Gershuny supports this when he states that women going out to work is leading to more shared household tasks. Also, women who work tend to do fewer household tasks than those who aren't in paid employment.
Ann Oakley criticised Young and Wilmott's view of the symmetrical view, claiming that men only had to complete a few of the household tasks in order for them to qualify as having integrated conjugal roles.	Caroline Gatrell found that women who work still complete most of the housework. Stephen Edgell further supports this in his study where he found that none of his sample families had joint conjugal roles.
The change in housework and childcare can be overstated.	The British Attitudes Survey also suggests that housework and childcare are still completed more by the female than the male partner. The results showed a very clear division of labour within households.
Duncombe and Marsden added the idea of emotional work to household labour.	Emotional work by the female has led to a triple shift of housework, paid work and emotional work. Dale Southerton supports this by claiming that it is the woman who has to plan and manage the family's quality time together.
New man/women as main earner. Unequal authority relations in the home between husband and wife.	An IPPR report in 2015 found that one-third of working mothers are the main breadwinner in their families. This is a large increase from twenty years ago.
There may be a 'crisis of masculinity'.	There is some concern in society that men are unsure of their identity and what it means to 'be male' due to the loss of traditional masculine jobs and the rise of women taking on the role of breadwinner in the family.

Is the functionalist view of conjugal roles positive?

Talcott Parsons believes there is a clear division of labour between spouses: the husband has an instrumental role whereas the wife has an expressive role.

Men and women have different and separate roles within the home as this is what society requires in order to run smoothly.

Young and Wilmott's study found that the family had become more equal and symmetrical.

Is the functionalist view of conjugal roles negative?

Marxists say that men and women have different roles as this is what capitalism requires in order to work effectively.

Marxists also believe the media supports this capitalist ideology through advertising campaigns and roles played in soap operas, etc.

There is no biological reason for the differences in conjugal roles.

Is the feminist view of conjugal roles positive?

Division of labour in a patriarchal society is not natural and only benefits men.

Delphy and Leonard believe in the idea of the dual burden – women have paid work outside the home and then have to do housework once they are home. This is further evidence of the exploitation of women.

Hannah Gavron believes that women have high expectations of marriage which lead to them feeling like their marriage is similar to a prison.

Is the feminist view of conjugal roles negative?

33 per cent of British people think mothers of pre-school age children should stay at home – this is a third of the population.

Functionalists and the New Right say that feminists focus too much on the negative side of the family.

It ignores the fact that some women actually enjoy and choose to take care of their children and running the family home.

REVISION BOOSTER

According to the British Social Attitudes Survey 2018, the gap between young and old in their views on gender roles has changed significantly. In 1991, 11 per cent of those aged 75 and over disagreed with the view that men should be breadwinners and women homemakers, compared with 67 per cent of people aged 18 to 34 years. By contrast, in 2017 47 per cent of those aged 75 and over say this, compared with 75 per cent of 18 to 34 year olds. This change in attitude will help to explain the move away from segregated conjugal roles to Young and Wilmott's idea of the symmetrical family.

Key figure

Hannah Gavron (1966) describes women as 'captive wives' as they feel that marriage is similar to being in a prison. She believes women feel 'captive' due to the unequal division of labour in the home going against their high expectations of marriage and freedom.

In the UK, men spend an average of 34 minutes on housework and cooking for every hour that women spend.

Knowledge check

1. Explain what is meant by 'the triple shift'. **(2 marks)**

2. Describe what Young and Wilmott mean by a 'symmetrical family'. **(4 marks)**

3. Describe the differences between integrated and segregated conjugal roles. **(8 marks)**

4. 'The family is still patriarchal.' Do you agree with this view? **(15 marks)**

Spec spotlight

2.3 Social changes and family relationships; changes in social norms, child-rearing patterns and child-centred families

Link to textbook
pp 64–65: The changing role of children

AO2 Apply

There are differences in experiences of childhood according to gender, class and ethnicity. Explain what factors could lead to this, giving examples.

Take it further

Sarah Womack has expressed lots of views on childhood and the experiences of children today. She believes that childhood now ends at 11 and that girls as young as 5 are worried about their shape and weight. How could you use Womack's findings in questions about Toxic Childhood and the March of Progress?

Childhood

Childhood is not just a stage of development but is socially constructed.	Childhood is not universal – different cultures have different norms and values. It is undergoing change and is perceived, by some, as threatened.
Legal changes have affected children and childhood.	Children now have a number of rights which are written into law, for example the UN Convention on the Rights of the Child. The 1989 Children's Act states that when parents divorce, the child must have a say in which parent they live with. Children are protected by law from corporal punishment, child abuse and child labour.
There has been growth of the child-centred family.	The position of children in the family has increased greatly over the last century. In many families it revolves around what the child wants and needs. More time and resources are dedicated to the children.
The reduction in completed family size has affected how children are treated.	As families have become smaller, they have become more child-centred.
The March of Progress view of childhood says that childhood has been steadily improving.	Childhood in the UK has improved over time. It is better today than in the past. Child labour has been outlawed. There is compulsory education for children. Children are more valued, protected, educated and have better health. Parents are less authoritarian and parent–child relationships are more democratic.

Modern childhood problems

Consumerism affects modern childhood.	Marxists see this as a negative aspect of child centredness. The media and advertisers target children who use pester power to get parents to buy products. This feeds the capitalist economy. David Buckingham states that children have become an important economic force.
Sue Palmer has worked on the problems of toxic childhood and mental health.	The current education system is putting children under more stress than the past. A recent survey by the Girl Guides claims that 69 per cent of girls and women aged between 11 and 21 state exams and tests are the main cause of stress in their lives.
	90 per cent of head teachers in a survey by ASCL say the new GCSEs have harmed pupils' mental health, triggering panic attacks, sleepless nights, self-harm and suicidal thoughts.
	A children's society report claims that 22 per cent of children aged 14 self-harmed in the last 12 months.
The rise of social media has affected stresses of childhood.	59 per cent of females between 11 and 21 said pressure from social media was another 'main cause of stress'.

There is plenty of research to support the theory that there is a link between greater amounts of screen time and childhood obesity.

Support for Sue Palmer's Toxic Childhood theory is:

In 2007 OFCOM banned advertising of junk food to children as a response to the problem of increasing childhood obesity.

Postman believes children are no longer innocent and free from responsibility and that the concept of childhood is disappearing. He blames TV for this, saying that children are not protected from the adult world.

It was estimated that in 2015 children spent on average six and a half hours a day on a screen compared with three hours in 1995.

Evidence against Sue Palmer's Toxic Childhood theory is:

Buckingham's research says that there is no evidence to suggest that TV advertising of junk food causes obesity.

Is this an example of a moral panic?

Sarah DeWatt believes that the demonization of screens is unfounded and that children can get many benefits, including education, and prompting conversation with their parents.

Support for the March of Progress view is:

Children are better educated – £64 billion is spent on education in the UK each year.

There are laws protecting children from child abuse and child labour.

Families are more child centred.

Evidence against of the March of Progress is:

It ignores the dark side of childhood – bullying, etc.

Child abuse still occurs – there are about 28,000 children on a child protection plan in the UK. The NSPCC estimates that 1 in 5 children are severely mistreated during their childhood.

There are inequalities among children in the UK in terms of opportunities.

Knowledge check

1. Describe what is meant by a 'child-centred' family.
   (2 marks)
2. Explain what sociologists mean by a 'Toxic Childhood'.
   (4 marks)
3. Explain how the relationship between parents and children has changed in the last 50 years. You should explore at least two reasons in your response. **(8 marks)**

REVISION BOOSTER

Womack says that children in the west are the most unhappy. Children in the UK have the poorest relationships with their parents and friends, experience more family breakdowns, suffer greater deprivation, and are exposed to more risks from alcohol, drugs and unsafe sex than any other wealthy country in the world. 3.7 million children were classified as living in poverty in 2012–13 in the UK. She also found that 31 per cent of children were physically abused by other children.

Key figures

Sue Palmer has worked on Toxic Childhood – the idea that children are being damaged by a combination of technology, decline of outdoor play, commercialisation of childhood and the competitive nature of the current education system. They eat more processed foods, parents fear paedophiles and abduction and there is an increase in obesity and mental health problems in children.

Philippe Aries claims the current idea of childhood is a relatively new development. It has only come about in the last 300 years. Previously childhood did not exist as a separate status. Children were seen as 'little adults' and took on the roles and responsibilities of adults as soon as they were physically able. However, **Linda Pollack** has criticised Aries for only using paintings for his evidence.

Molly Russell, a 14-year-old school girl, took her own life in 2017. Her family found worrying material on her Instagram account about depression and suicide. Is this an example which supports Sue Palmer's Toxic Childhood Theory?

Spec spotlight

2.4 Sociological theories of the role of the family

Link to textbook

pp 72–73: The Marxist view of the family

pp 74–77: The feminist view of the family

pp 78–79: A summary of sociological theories on the family

AO2 Apply

Research the five types of family that the Rapoports describe. Write a sentence explaining each type in your own words.

Take it further

Compare the consensus view of functionalism and the conflict views of feminism and Marxism regarding the family. What do they say? What are the criticisms of each one? Which do you agree with more and why?

Functionalists believe that the family is the basic building block of society.

Different theories of the family

Functionalist	Just like an organ in the human body, functionalists believe that the family enables society to function. The family is the basic building block of society which helps to maintain social order and cohesion.
	Talcott Parsons describes two key functions of the family: 1) primary socialisation and 2) stabilisation of adult personality.
	Murdock says that the family performs four essential functions to meet the needs of society and its members.
New Right	The traditional nuclear family and its values are best for society. Both children and the wider society benefit from stable families who have traditional conjugal roles.
	The increase in lone-parent and reconstituted families lead to an increase in social problems including crime.
Marxist	The family meets the needs of capitalism, not the needs of family members and society as a whole. This helps to maintain class inequality. The three functions that the family has to promote capitalism are: 1) inheritance of property, 2) ideological functions and 3) unit of consumption (advertisers urge families to 'keep up with the Jones' by consuming all the latest products, the media target children who use 'pester power' to persuade parents to buy more).
	Friedrich Engels believed the family developed so men could control women and children and allow them to pass their property to their offspring.
Feminist	The nuclear family is patriarchal, serves the needs of men and is repressive. Men benefit from families at the expense of women.
	Delphy and Leonard are radical feminists who say that the family is patriarchal because: 1) women are exploited economically – labour is used by their husbands, 2) family is hierarchal, with men at the top and 3) patriarchal family reflects patriarchal society.
Postmodernist	Family structures are varied. There is no longer one dominant family type. Family diversity is now the norm.
	People have more choice.

Support for the Marxist view of the family is:

Engels believes that marriage occurs in order for property to be passed to the right heirs. The family has an economic function.

The family reproduces the inequality in society as it helps the capitalist economy. The family buys products and this benefits the bourgeoisie as they make the profit.

Zaretsky believes that the family as an institution makes sure that capitalism continues as it is a consumer of the products of capitalism and makes a profit for the bourgeoisie.

Evidence against the Marxist view of the family is:

The Marxist view ignores other reasons for getting married such as forming a family. There is also no direct evidence to support Engel's view.

Women are becoming increasingly financially independent and no longer rely on men for financial reasons in the same way as in the past.

This theory assumes that the breadwinner is male and that all women are housewives. This does not apply to all families in the UK.

Support for the feminist view of the family is:

Delphy and Leonard say that the family is a patriarchal institution where men dominate and exploit women.

Greer found that men get more out of marriage than women – single women are more likely to be happier than married women.

Ann Oakley criticises Young and Wilmott's theory of the symmetrical family – she found that while 72 per cent of men now claim to help with housework, this could mean only doing one task.

Evidence against the feminist view of the family is:

Families with dual worker couples may be equal. More women are financially independent and have more power in the family than some feminists may suggest.

Hakim says that women's inequality in the family may be their own personal choice. Women may choose to be a housewife as they enjoy it.

Feminism assumes that all families are patriarchal and that all women are subservient.

Perspective	Criticism
Functionalist	Criticisms of Murdock – other institutions and family types can carry out the functions.
Marxist	Ignores family diversity and the fact that women work.
	Ignores the benefits of the nuclear family, for example, both parents support the children.
Feminist	Ignores the diversity of modern family life assuming that everyone lives in heterosexual, nuclear families.
	Paints a very negative picture of family life – possibly exaggerated.
	Women are portrayed as passive victims of exploitation.
Postmodernist	The amount of social change experienced in society is exaggerated.
	Chester – most adults still marry and have children. Most children are raised by their natural parents. Most people live in a household shared by a married, heterosexual couple. Most marriages continue until death.
New Right	Findings are not cross checked. Two or more methods can help this to be sure of research findings.
	A fuller picture can be obtained with both reliability and validity. Eileen Barker used the unstructured interviews to help create hypotheses for her participant observation.

Think link

Although this revision spread is about the different sociological perspectives on the family, try to also think of ways of bringing in gender and the family and how they are linked.

Key figure

Ann Oakley is a feminist who analyses the 'conventional family', finding: 1) women are expected to do unpaid work, 2) the idea of the conventional family is powerful, 3) people expect happiness, but nuclear family can be stressful and 4) there is more family diversity in the middle class. Symmetrical family is a myth, women still do most of the housework.

Knowledge check

1. Describe what is meant by the traditional nuclear family. **(2 marks)**
2. Explain why functionalists argue that nuclear families are important. **(4 marks)**
3. 'The family is good for its members and for society.' Do you agree with this view? **(15 marks)**
4. 'The main purpose of the family is to reinforce and maintain capitalism.' Do you agree with this view? **(15 marks)**

Spec spotlight

3.2 Processes inside school affecting educational achievement

3.3 Patterns of educational achievement: patterns of attainment by social class

3.4 Factors affecting educational achievement: social class

Link to textbook

pp 82–83: Differences in attainment between social classes

Why does attending a public school such as Eton College give you a higher chance of attending Oxbridge?

AO2 Apply

For each of the inside and outside school factors, write a couple of sentences explaining how that particular factor has an impact on a pupil's educational achievement. Which of the factors do you think has the biggest impact? Explain the reasons leading you to think this.

Take it further

There has been a study recently by the Institute of Fiscal Studies which claims that children from more disadvantaged backgrounds have more spent on their education by the government than middle-class pupils. This is because of the introduction of government initiatives such as the Pupil Premium, which gives schools additional money for those children who are entitled to free school meals due to a low income. Why is this the case? What effect could this have on educational achievement?

How does social class affect educational achievement?

Some sociologists argue that working-class underachievement is caused by an inadequacy in working-class culture.	Poverty is a cause of educational underachievement, for example, lack of basic resources. The new reformed GCSEs have widened the gap further between disadvantaged pupils and their peers.
Pupils from professional backgrounds are more likely to enter further and higher education.	According to the Sutton Trust, Eton (a top public school) sent 211 pupils to Oxbridge over a three-year period, while over 1300 state schools sent no pupils to any top universities.
Stephen Aldridge found that middle-class children have higher achievements at school than working-class children with the same IQ.	Pupils from working-class backgrounds are more likely to study vocational subjects whereas middle-class pupils are more likely to study A Levels. Pupils from disadvantaged backgrounds are less likely to start school being able to read.
A recent study by UCL and Kings' College London found that class background is the most crucial factor when determining academic success.	This study compared the GCSE grades of pupils in more affluent areas of the country with more deprived areas and found that the middle-class pupils attained higher grades regardless of whether they were in an affluent or deprived area.

Why do working-class pupils not match the achievements of middle-class pupils? Inside school factors

Preconceptions and school structures can affect working-class children before they even start studying.	Working-class pupils may be labelled negatively according to stereotypes held by the teachers. This can then lead to self-fulfilling prophecy. Stephen Ball found that pupils in the top bands were from higher social classes.
Anti-school subcultures, as discussed by Paul Willis, can be important.	Working-class pupils can feel marginalised and looked down upon by teachers and then look down on themselves – this, in turn, can affect their school performance.
The quality of schools and type of school attended can have an effect.	There are failings within the education system itself – for example, many underperforming schools are found in predominantly working-class areas.
Teacher retention can have a negative effect. As there is a national shortage of teachers in this country at the moment, teachers may prefer to teach in a more middle-class school which could be deemed as 'easier'.	According to Howard Becker, teachers are often middle class and therefore can see middle-class pupils as 'ideal'. This example of labelling can lead to working-class pupils believing that they are not good enough and therefore has an impact on their educational achievement.

Why do working-class pupils not match the achievements of middle-class pupils? Outside school factors

Material deprivation and financial disadvantage can mean pupils lack the basic resources needed – for example, books, revision guides and money for educational trips.	Barry Sugarman believes that middle-class pupils understand the benefits of deferred gratification whereas working-class pupils prefer immediate gratification. They get the rewards immediately and therefore may leave school at the earliest opportunity in order to earn money.
Working-class parents may have lower expectations for their children and place a lower value on education than middle-class parents.	There may be an element of fatalism which affects their achievement – working-class pupils may feel that they are not likely to achieve in their education and this, in turn, leads to self-fulfilling prophecy.

Cultural deprivation is another way in which working-class pupils can be negatively affected.

Working-class pupils may not be taken to museums and art galleries or discuss current affairs and politics at home as much – this lack of cultural capital puts them at a disadvantage.

Basil Bernstein believes that working-class pupils use a 'restricted code' rather than the elaborated code of the middle class.

This puts them at a disadvantage when communicating with teachers and accessing texts and exam papers, etc. Working-class children are also less likely to attend nursery which means they are missing out on the basics of education from the start.

AO3
Evaluation

Support for the argument that social class affects educational achievement is:

A 2000 OFSTED report showed that the impact of social class on educational achievement was more than twice as great as that of ethnicity.

In 2015/2016 pupils eligible for free school meals were less likely to achieve A* to C in English and Maths GCSE than those not eligible: 39 per cent versus 67 per cent.

Pupils from lower-class backgrounds on average achieve lower scores on SATs and GCSEs and are more likely to be placed in lower streams or bands.

Pupils eligible for free school meals are less likely to attend university or attend the top ones.

Evidence against the argument that social class affects educational achievement is:

It does not take into account ethnicity and gender.

It does not take into account compensatory education schemes (e.g. Pupil Premium).

Interactionists would argue that this argument ignores the effect of labelling by teachers.

It fails to take into account the concept of meritocracy.

Working-class culture is different not deficient.

Hans Eysenck believes it is difficult to be sure if it is IQ or social factors which determine educational achievement.

Key figures

Helen Connor and **Sara Dewson** found that working-class families have a need for immediate gratification; therefore they opt out of higher education. Middle-class families defer gratification because they can support their children – this means they are more likely to go on to university. This also ties in with the idea of cultural capital.

Think link

When discussing social class and educational achievement, try to also think of ways of bringing in ethnicity and gender and how they are linked. Social class differences should not really be considered in isolation from gender and/or ethnicity.

REVISION BOOSTER

Recent research by the Sutton Trust has found that good parenting, parental engagement and stimulating home environment have more of an impact on achievement than the income a family receives. Reading to children every day, having a regular bedtime routine and good parenting can overcome some of the impact that a low family income can have on a child's educational attainment.

Does a pupil's social class have an effect on their exam results?

Knowledge check

1. Describe what is meant by immediate gratification.　**(2 marks)**

2. Explain two ways in which a pupil's home background could influence their achievement at school.　**(4 marks)**

3. Identify two factors inside school which could affect a working-class pupil's achievement.　**(4 marks)**

4. 'Social class is the biggest influence on a pupil's educational achievement.' Is this statement accurate? In your answer you are advised to refer to material and any other relevant factors to support your judgement.　**(15 marks)**

Cultural deprivation, cultural capital and cultural factors

Spec spotlight

3.3 Patterns of educational achievement: patterns of attainment by social class

3.4 Factors affecting educational achievement: cultural factors

Link to textbook
pp 84–87: The importance of cultural factors
pp 90–91: The importance of schools and what goes on inside them

AO2 Apply

What does Basil Bernstein mean when he talks about the restricted code and the elaborated code? How do the differences between working-class and middle-class language affect educational achievement?

What advantages do middle-class children have as a result of their social background?

Take it further

Look up where your local children's centre is. What activities and courses take place there? Who is eligible to attend? Which areas of families' lives do children's centres focus on? How does the work of the children's centre help to combat the effects of cultural and material deprivation?

Think link
Although this revision spread is about cultural deprivation, try to also think of ways of bringing in the differences in educational achievement between the different social classes, material deprivation and ethnicity.

Cultural deprivation

Sociologists believe that cultural differences may affect attainment.	Cultural deprivation is the idea that working-class children fail because their values are inferior to those of middle-class children – that working-class culture is not aimed at educational success.
A 2007 study from the Centre for Longitudinal Studies found that by the age of three, children from less advantaged backgrounds are already a year behind those from more advantaged backgrounds.	The gap continues to widen as they get older. Many sociologists would argue that this is because of cultural deprivation.

Cultural factors inside school

Anti-school subcultures, as shown by Paul Willis, can have a negative effect.	High-achieving pupils in working-class schools may be bullied because of their success.
Setting and streaming can also have an effect.	Working-class children can be labelled as 'stupid' – this can lead to self-fulfilling prophecy.
The education system is mainly controlled by middle-class people.	Tests are seen as created for the middle class – for example, the 11+ is criticised for being too biased towards middle class. Schools tend to teach the cultural capital of middle class; for example, classical music.

Cultural factors outside school

J. W. B. Douglas says that parental interest is the most important factor in affecting achievement.	It is argued that middle-class parents expect more from their children and are more interested in their progress. Middle-class parents are more likely to attend open evenings.
Middle-class parents have knowledge of how to 'work the system'.	They can hold their own in disagreements with teachers about the teaching of their children, knowing what books to buy, etc.
Cultural capital is more likely to be obtained in middle-class families.	Middle-class pupils are more likely to be taken to the library, museums, trips out, have books at home. Middle-class children are more likely to have parents who read the broadsheets, and appreciate and discuss the arts.

Are middle-class parents more likely to help their children with their homework and their studies?

Support for the argument that working-class culture affects educational achievement is:

Sue Palmer and Melanie Phillips support this by saying that working-class people are not good at parenting. They transmit values that cause children to fail in school.	Douglas claims that working-class parents may be less likely to attend parents' evenings.	Working-class children struggle to adapt to the middle-class norms and values found in schools.

Evidence against the argument that working-class culture affects educational achievement is:

Working-class parents may be less likely to attend open evenings and parents' evenings because they have to work inconvenient shifts rather than they simply do not wish to attend.	Working-class parents may have had negative school experiences and this has an effect on their desire to attend events such as parents' evenings.	Postmodernists argue that there is no longer a distinct working class.
Marxists would say that the working class are actually victims of social inequality rather than the cause of their children's educational underachievement.	A number of schools with mainly working-class pupils have less effective systems of parent and school communication and contact.	

Support for the argument that cultural deprivation affects educational achievement is:

Middle-class parents are more likely to take their children to museums and art galleries, etc.	Middle-class parents are more likely to read the broadsheets and discuss current affairs with their children.	Middle-class parenting styles emphasise the importance of education more than working-class culture.

Evidence against the argument that cultural deprivation affects educational achievement is:

Nell Keddie describes 'cultural deprivation' as a myth and says that working-class pupils are culturally different rather than culturally deprived.	This theory treats working-class culture as inferior whereas many people would say it is just different.	It fails to take into account the links with material deprivation.

Strengths of Basil Bernstein's argument that class differences in speech patterns affects educational achievement are:

The elaborated code used by the middle classes is the language used by teachers – this puts middle-class pupils at an advantage.	Language is important for success at school, both spoken and written.	'Correct' English is expected and praised and, as middle-class children are more likely to have been brought up using and seeing this as the norm, they will probably find settling and doing what is required easier.

Weaknesses of Basil Bernstein's argument that class differences in speech patterns affects educational achievement are:

He ignores variety and variations within the different social classes.	He does not have much evidence to support his theory.	He assumes all of the middle class speak in elaborated code.

AO2 Apply

The children's TV programme Sesame Street came out of an American compensatory education initiative. Find out what the aims were and what skills it wanted to develop in poorer children. Was Sesame Street an effective form of compensatory education? What do critics of the scheme say?

Take it further

Diane Reay has written a book, *Miseducation: Inequality, education and the working classes*, about the inequality between the classes in the British education system. She believes that working-class children get less of an education than middle-class pupils – even if they are in the same school in the same building. Reay would be a great person to use in an essay on class and educational achievement and/or material deprivation and education. Read some of her interviews or her book and make sure you include a few sentences about her research and findings in your exam answer.

How can material deprivation affect educational achievement? Inside school factors

Working-class children may underachieve in comparison with middle-class children due to lack of resources and money.	Research from UCL found that the average primary-aged pupil in private education has £12,000 a year spent on their education compared to £4800 per year on the average state pupil. This can mean bigger class sizes and fewer resources.
Lack of school funding can also affect what schools can provide outside school hours.	Many working-class areas, such as in the inner cities, may lack pre-school facilities.
Schools in poorer areas tend to have poorer facilities and a higher turnover of staff. Research has found that this can have a negative effect on a child's development.	Jan Flaherty found that material deprivation and financial issues were an important factor in younger children's poor attendance at school. In 2006 only 33 per cent of children receiving free school meals gained five or more GCSEs at A*–C, compared to 61 per cent of pupils not receiving free school meals.

How can material deprivation affect educational achievement? Outside school factors

Working-class pupils may underachieve due to lack of resources and money.	They may have no computer or internet access, no educational toys or books and cannot afford private tutors. Poor diet may make them ill and lead to absence.
Older students may need to take a job while studying. Tess Ridge found that children from poorer backgrounds take on jobs such as babysitting and paper rounds.	Helen Connor and Sara Dewson found that working-class children fear being a burden on already overstretched families so go to work, which leaves them less time to study.
Housing can have a detrimental effect.	Their choice of school may be limited by where they live – selection by mortgage. They may live in housing with no adequate study area – overcrowding can mean nowhere to study or complete their homework. Poor housing can lead to illness and absence from school, e.g. from damp or cold conditions.
Pupils from more advantaged backgrounds can afford to attend the better universities.	For example, Coventry is 15–19 per cent more expensive to live in than the average city in the UK but middle-class parents are willing to pay that to enable their children to attend Warwick University.

Does the ability to pay for a private tutor give a child an advantage?

Support for the argument that material deprivation affects educational achievement is:		
A. Gibson and S. Asthana say there is a link between low household income and poor educational achievement.	Children from less advantaged backgrounds cannot afford a private tutor or private schooling.	Payne says that middle-class parents of A Level students can and do pay for private tuition for their children.
Low-income families can't afford to support their children through university.	Halsey says that the main reason why working-class pupils do not stay on at school is lack of financial support.	J. W. B. Douglas found that children who live in unsatisfactory conditions don't do as well in school tests as those from wealthier backgrounds.

Sesame Street was originally designed as a form of compensatory education.

Evidence against the argument that material deprivation affects educational achievement is:		
Many children from poor backgrounds do achieve highly in education.	Educated parents, regardless of income, will encourage and motivate their children to do well.	Compensatory education can help reduce the negative impact of material deprivation.
It is too deterministic.	It does not take into account other factors such as cultural deprivation.	Pupil Premium has been introduced by the government to help children from families with a lower income.

Why are the children of middle-class parents and higher social classes more likely to attend university?

REVISION BOOSTER

Further research – Alasdair Forsyth and Andy Furlong's study about why poorer students are more likely to drop out of university. What other factors do they suggest contribute to this disadvantage? What are some of the criticisms of this study?

Key figures

Alasdair Forsyth and **Andy Furlong** of Glasgow University looked at what the barriers were for working-class pupils in education. They found that it is the fear of debt, constant money worries and the cost of education that prevents working-class pupils going on to higher education. They look at the 'hidden costs' (uniforms, trips, books, equipment, etc.). Working-class students may need to juggle part-time work with studying and may worry about repaying this debt once they finish their course. This puts them at a disadvantage in their education.

Knowledge check

1. Describe what is meant by 'income'.
   (2 marks)
2. Describe what is meant by 'material deprivation'.
   (2 marks)
3. Explain two reasons why children of middle-class parents are more likely to go on to higher education than children of working-class parents. (8 marks)
4. 'Home and family have the greatest influence on a student's educational achievement.' Do you agree? Why? (15 marks)

Spec spotlight

3.2 Processes inside school affecting educational achievement: labelling, including the work of Hargreaves

Link to textbook

pp 92–93: Teacher expectations and labelling

pp 94–95: The effects of teacher labelling on achievement

AO2 Apply

Research Robert Rosenthal and Lenore Jacobson's study 'Pygmalion in the Classroom'. The aim of this study was to test the theory of self-fulfilling prophecy. What were the findings of the study? How can you use this study in an exam question about labelling, self-fulfilling prophecy and teachers' expectations?

Take it further

What is meant by the 'halo effect'? How can this put middle-class pupils who are not as bright at an advantage over bright working-class pupils?

Do teachers label the pupils in their classroom?

What is labelling theory?

Howard Becker came up with the idea of labelling theory. It is an interactionist theory which helps to explain underachievement in education.

Labelling theory is the idea that people are given labels and then other people act as though those labels are true. These labels can affect our behaviour.

Becker says that labelling theory is how the identity and behaviour of an individual is categorised and described by others in their society.

In other words, it is to attach a meaning or definition to somebody, for example, Emily is a bright pupil or Grace is a troublemaker.

Studies show that teachers may label pupils based on stereotypes based on their class, ethnicity, gender, etc.

Becker interviewed 60 Chicago high school teachers and found that they judged pupils in their classes according to how closely they fitted an image of the 'ideal pupil'. They looked at a pupil's appearance, personality, speech and social class. Teachers saw middle-class children as closest to the 'ideal'.

How are labelling and ethnicity linked?

Cecile Wright found evidence that teachers in primary schools viewed and therefore treated children from non-white ethnic minorities differently from white children. David Gillborn found similar results in secondary schools.

African-Caribbean boys were more likely to be labelled as aggressive and Asian children were more likely to be labelled as a 'problem'. David Gilborn found that teachers negatively label black students.

However, not all pupils live up to their expectations.

Mary Fuller found that black girls in a comprehensive school rejected the negative labels applied to them, worked extremely hard and were successful. This is an example of self-negating prophecy which is where the pupils refuse to accept the label that the teacher has applied on them, and instead uses the support of others such as parents or other teachers to prove the teacher wrong.

What is self-fulfilling prophecy?

Self-fulfilling prophecy is the idea that something becomes true because someone said that it would happen.

Once a negative label is applied to a individual, they live up the expectation of the given label. Expectations of pupils made by teachers tend to come true.

For example, Thomas may come from a working-class family and as such the teachers may stereotype him as not being as bright as another pupil who is from a middle-class family.

Thomas may become demotivated and not see any point in working hard at school. He may not behave well at school as he has been labelled as 'naughty'. This could lead to Thomas being placed in lower sets at school where he is not given the same work as those in the higher sets and where the expectations are lower. Thomas believes that he will never achieve at school. so Thomas leaves school with no GCSEs.

Support for the argument that labelling affects educational achievement is:		
Labelling can affect a pupil's attitudes towards school, their behaviour, and ultimately their level of achievement in education.	Teachers may form stereotypes of their ideal pupil and treat pupils differently depending on how they view them.	Negative labelling can mean that pupils get placed in lower sets or streams. Stephen Ball found that the pupils in the higher sets were more likely to be from middle-class backgrounds.
Teachers may praise some pupils more and others less, they may give them easier or more difficult tasks or have higher or lower expectations of the pupil based on the label they have given them.	Ray Rist completed a study where he observed a teacher who used the pupils' home background and appearance to place them in groups. The more middle-class pupils were placed in a group nearer to the teacher and given more encouragement, the more working-class pupils were seated further away from the teacher and given lower-ability reading material.	

Evidence against the argument that labelling affects educational achievement is:		
Not all teachers view middle-class pupils as the 'ideal' pupil, as Becker claimed to find.	A study by Amelia Hempel-Jorgensen found that these ideas of the 'ideal' pupil differ according to the social class of the school. In a mainly working-class school the ideal pupil was defined as quiet, passive and obedient, whereas, in a mainly middle-class school the ideal pupil was defined in terms of their personality and academic ability rather than by their behaviour.	Labelling and self-fulfilling prophecy don't explain how other factors such as poverty and cultural deprivation can also have an impact on educational achievement.
Some sociologists argue that labelling theory is too deterministic. Fuller's study above and the concept of self-negating prophecy help to support this.	Even if teachers do have an 'ideal' pupil this theory doesn't explain why teachers hold by these stereotypes in the first place.	There have been questions raised as to the quality and administration of the Rosenthal and Jacobson study.

Can labelling lead to self-fulfilling prophecy?

Think link
Try to think of ways of bringing in social class, ethnicity, gender and anti-school subculture when writing about labelling and self-fulfilling prophecy.

Key figure

David Hargreaves studied teachers in two secondary schools. He believes they made judgements about students based on their behaviour, ability and potential. As these students had only recently arrived at the school they had little information on which to form these judgements and he believes they based their ideas mainly on the area that they came from. These first impressions over time became labels which, in turn, could lead to a self-fulfilling prophecy.

Knowledge check

1. Describe what is meant by 'self-fulfilling prophecy'. **(2 marks)**
2. Explain how the labelling theory could lead to self-fulfilling prophecy. **(4 marks)**
3. Explain two reasons why the labelling theory could lead to pupils underachieving in education. **(5 marks)**
4. "Labelling a pupil negatively will always lead to underachievement." Do you agree with this view? **(15 marks)**

Spec spotlight

3.2 Processes inside school affecting educational achievement

3.3 Patterns of educational achievement: patterns of attainment by ethnicity

3.4 Factors affecting educational achievement: ethnicity

Link to textbook

pp 96–101: Differences in attainment in ethnic groups

AO2 Apply

Look at the charts showing the percentage of pupils attaining A* to C in English and Maths GCSE by ethnicity found at https://www.ethnicity-facts-figures. service.gov.uk/education-skills- and-training/11-to-16-years-old/ percentage-achieving-a-c-in- english-and-maths/latest.

What can you learn from them? What questions might sociologists want to ask after looking at these charts? What are some of the possible answers to these questions?

Take it further

A recent study by UCL indicates that black pupils are more likely than white pupils to be in the bottom sets for Maths. Using your knowledge on class, ethnicity, labelling and streaming explain why some researchers believe that this is evidence that institutional racism still exists today in schools.

Ethnic background and differences in educational achievement

A child's ethnicity can affect their educational achievement.

Generally, children from Indian and Chinese backgrounds achieve higher at school than other ethnicities. In 2015–16, Chinese pupils were most likely to achieve A*–C in GCSE Maths and English whereas Gypsy/Roma pupils were the least likely. Bangladeshi and West Indian children tend to underperform.

Students from some ethnic minority groups in Britain, such as Chinese, Indian, Black African and Bangladeshi have significantly improved their grades over the last two decades.

They are achieving higher than the national averages, pointing to improving social mobility from ethnic groups who have traditionally struggled to get good grades at GCSE.

Outside school factors	Inside school factors
Social class, language spoken at home, parental expectations, material deprivation/poverty, cultural deprivation, lack of male role models due to higher rate of lone-parent families in African-Caribbean families	Labelling, teacher expectations, hidden curriculum, racism, Black teachers under represented, ethnocentric curriculum, possible anti-school subculture

Reasons for different levels of educational achievement

There can be different expectations of different ethnic minority groups – this is linked to labelling theory.

According to David Gillborn teachers may negatively label black students. African-Caribbean children can be seen as a challenge to authority and are more likely to be excluded. They can be seen as less academic than children from other ethnic backgrounds. Teachers expect less, so black pupils are not as encouraged as others.

In contrast, teachers may hold high expectations of Asian students as they can be considered to be more capable and hard working.

Both can lead to self-fulfilling prophecies.

Hidden/ethnocentric curriculum – schools are structured in a particular way including such aspects as school assemblies, history and language which reflect the culture of the majority.

The curriculum fits white, middle-class cultures. Students learn European languages, history lessons are focused on that culture, school holidays fit around certain times, especially religious festivals.

Textbooks may have stereotypical views or ignore contributions of black people.

IQ tests can be ethnocentric – sometimes they ask things that aren't a test of your IQ but are a test of cultural knowledge.

However, with the increase of multiculturalism some things may have got better – for example, more coverage of different cultures.

Teachers from ethnic minorities are significantly under represented in schools.

There are fewer role models and they are less likely to be in positions of authority. Ethnic minority teachers may be confined to teaching certain subjects, for example, offering language support to classroom teachers. This may give the impression that school is a 'white' experience, so limiting their chance of success.

Policies and attitudes of the school may be racist. This can include both intentional and unintentional racism.

This attitude can come from teachers as well as other students. As a result of teacher's attitudes, some black students may be more likely to be placed in lower sets or streams and to be entered for lower level papers.

There is also the role of discrimination in setting – ethnic minorities are more likely to be in lower sets.

Many ethnic groups are in lower social classes so suffer material deprivation associated with the lower classes, such as poor housing and lack of resources.

For example, the Bangladeshi children who underachieved tended, on average, to be from poorer homes.

Support for the argument that ethnicity affects educational achievement is:

Some ethnic minority groups perform really well at GCSE and A level whereas other ethnic minority groups underperform.

In 2018, on average, pupils from the Chinese, Asian and mixed ethnic groups scored higher than the national average for Attainment 8.

In 2018, white pupils and black pupils scored below the national average for Attainment 8.

In 2018, pupils from the Gypsy/Roma and Irish Traveller ethnic groups had the lowest average score for Attainment 8.

Evidence against the argument that ethnicity affects educational achievement is:

Pupils eligible for free school meals from Indian, Chinese and Bangladeshi backgrounds are performing higher than white students on free school meals.

Margaret Fuller found that African-Caribbean girls in London resisted negative labelling and worked hard to gain success.

Some schools in working-class inner-city areas have a lot of ethnic minority students enrolled. These may not do as well as schools in more middle-class areas that may attract better quality teachers, have better resources and higher levels of parental support. It might be that it is social class rather than ethnicity that is the crucial factor here.

Support for the argument that language differences affects educational achievement is:

Language can be a problem for immigrant families when they first arrive in UK.

For many children from immigrant homes, the main language of the home is generally the country of origin. Therefore, their studies are carried out in a 'foreign' language.

Carl Bereiter and Siegfried Engelmann say that language is a major barrier in educational achievement.

Evidence against the argument that language differences affects educational achievement is:

Saeeda Shah of Leicester University says that some ethnic minority children may start school with limited English vocabulary as it is not spoken in their homes, but once in school they develop language quickly and then they appear to make more rapid progress in educational achievement compared to white British pupils.

The Swann Report says that language is not a major factor in educational achievement.

Heidi Mirza says that Indian children do very well despite often not having English as their home language.

Support for the argument that parental expectations affect educational achievement is:

It can be argued that parents from some ethnic minority groups are less interested in their children's education than parents from other groups.

Some sociologists believe that some black children are raised with a fatalistic attitude.

Some sociologists believe that some ethnic minorities do not value education.

Evidence against the argument that parental expectations affect educational achievement is:

A study by the Inner London Education Authority reported that Indian families put pressure on their children to succeed and this has affected their performance in a positive way.

In a number of areas, African-Caribbean parents set up Saturday schools as they were worried about their child's underachievement.

According to Ken Pryce, African-Caribbean parents have very high aspirations for their children.

Ghazali Bhatti states that for some Asian parents, who were often poorly educated themselves, there was a strong desire to help their children's education more.

Many parents from ethnic minority families make sacrifices to pay for private tutoring of their children despite limited resources.

Key figure

Cecile Wright says Asian children may be excluded from classroom discussions and therefore discriminated against due to teachers' assumptions about their level of English. African-Caribbean males may receive more negative attention from teachers than their white peers. All of this will contribute to pupils from an ethnic minority background being at a disadvantage in education.

Think link

When writing about ethnicity, try to think of ways of bringing in social class, as this is closely linked to ethnicity. Think about the impact of free school meals eligibility and material deprivation and how they are closely linked to ethnicity and educational achievement.

Knowledge check

1. Describe what is meant by ethnocentric. **(2 marks)**
2. Explain two reasons why pupils from ethnic minorities may join or form an anti-school subculture. **(4 marks)**
3. Outline ways in which parental values and ethnicity can influence a child's attitude to education. **(8 marks)**
4. 'Inside school factors are the main cause of differences in the educational achievement of pupils of different ethnicities.' Do you agree? Why? **(15 marks)**

Link to textbook

pp 102–103: Anti-school subcultures

AO2 Apply

Do anti-school subcultures exist in your school? Can you identify any groups of pupils who may have rejected education and the authority of the teachers? How do they behave? Which social class would you associate them with?

Take it further

Paul Willis is a neo-Marxist sociologist who holds the view that the education system is biased against working-class pupils. He wrote a book called *Learning to Labour: How Working Class Kids Get Working Class Jobs*. In his study, he observed twelve working-class boys at school. He also observed their fathers at work and found that the boys' behaviour and attitude mirrored that of their fathers. Read further about Willis' study and jot down what you find in your research – this will be very useful in an exam question on education and social class.

What is an anti-school subculture?

This is a group within a school which rejects education and the authority of the teachers.	They do not value or see the point of education and will go against the norms and values of the school.
Why would a child form or join an anti-school subculture?	This may be a reaction to the negative labelling they feel they receive at school. They can gain status amongst their friends by being rude or badly behaved, truanting or 'acting the clown'. This is a way of rebelling against a system which is telling them that they are not going to achieve. Paul Lacey researched the effects of being placed in lower sets and found that streaming can lead to pupils forming anti-school subcultures.
How does belonging to an anti-school subculture affect educational achievement?	Those who join an anti-school subculture can reject the values of the school, disrupt lessons and truant. This means they cannot achieve success in their education and will leave school with little or no qualifications.

Support for the argument that anti-school subcultures affect educational achievement is:

Status is earned by disrupting lessons and avoiding school work.

Colin Lacey found that boys in lower streams tended to reject standards of behaviour expected by the school, which had labelled them as 'failures'.

David Hargreaves found that pupils in lower sets at were labelled as 'troublemakers' and rebelled against the values of the school.

Máirtín Mac an Ghaill taught in two inner-city colleges. He found that African-Caribbean boys formed anti-school subcultures as a reaction against the institutional racism they experienced while at college.

Evidence against the argument that anti-school subcultures affect educational achievement is:

Tony Sewell believes that only a minority of African-Caribbean boys have an anti-school subculture.

Peter Woods suggests that pupils switch between pro, anti-school subcultures and other variations during their school year.

Support for Paul Willis' study to demonstrate that anti-school subcultures affect educational achievement is:

'The lads' saw school as being for middle-class children.

'The lads' were not interested in school and were only interested in 'having a laff'.

This study can be relevant today when looking at NEETs and the underachievement of white, working-class boys.

Evidence against Paul Willis' study to demonstrate that anti-school subcultures affect educational achievement is:

There are a number of ethical issues. For example, Willis witnessed the lads getting into fights, being racist and vandalising school property yet did nothing about it.

Willis used a small sample size of just 12 white boys – the representativeness is poor.

It is not reliable as it would be hard to replicate this study today.

It is an outdated study.

Some people think Willis has romanticised these lads as 'working-class heroes' when in fact they were sexist and anti-social.

REVISION BOOSTER

In contrast to the anti-school subculture, some pupils who accept and follow the school rules and attend regularly form a pro-school subculture. These pupils who conform and are positive about school may be regarded as the 'ideal' pupils by the teachers. A self-fulfilling prophecy may occur as these students gain status from their peers and teachers for working hard, behaving well and achieving academic success.

Think link
Try to think of ways to bring social class in relation to educational achievement and subcultures in schools into your answers.

Key figure

Paul Willis studied a group of boys in a comprehensive school who called themselves 'the lads'. They rejected school and its values and seemed only interested in leaving school as soon as they could. They were only interested in 'having a laff' and, as such, disrupted lessons, behaved badly and bullied those students who wanted to work hard and do well. 'The lads' were able to gain status amongst their peers by forming this anti-school subculture and behaving in the way described above. This is the most well-known study when looking at anti-school subculture.

Knowledge check

1. Describe what is meant by an 'anti-school subculture'. **(2 marks)**
2. Explain, using examples, why some pupils form anti-school subcultures. **(8 marks)**

Spec spotlight

3.1 Sociological theories of the role of education: feminist theory of education perpetuating patriarchy

3.3 Patterns of educational achievement: patterns of attainment by gender

3.5 Factors affecting educational achievement: gender

Link to textbook

pp 106–109: Differences in attainment between boys and girls

AO2 Apply

The government has introduced a number of initiatives and policies to increase the numbers of women in STEM subjects and careers. Examples include WISE and GIST. Find out what these initiatives do to encourage more females into STEM and how successful they are.

Take it further

There is a 13 per cent pay gap between male and female leaders in schools today. What factors may contribute to this? What effect could this on the educational achievement of girls?

Initiatives such as GIST and WISE have tried to encourage more females into careers in fields such as science and technology.

Girls and STEM subjects

STEM is Science, Technology, Engineering and Maths.	The disparity in the number of boys and girls studying STEM subjects needs to be addressed in order for females to have an equal chance in the ever-changing job market. A recent study from the Social Mobility Foundation indicates that science and technology jobs will grow twice as fast as other jobs. If the gap isn't narrowed then there is concern that the UK will have a skills gap and, in turn, the economy could be affected.
A recent study at Dundee University found that there is virtually no difference between girls and boys when it comes to attainment.	Instead, the problem is the 'gendering of STEM subjects'. A Level results in 2018 showed that girls are more likely to drop STEM subjects after GCSE – girls completed 55 per cent of the A Levels taken in 2018 yet only 43 per cent of A Levels in STEM subjects were completed by girls.
Women are under-represented in STEM occupations.	About half of the workforce in the UK are female yet they make up only 14.4 per cent of people working in STEM occupations.

Why are boys underachieving compared with girls?

Harris says that boys are thought to be suffering increasingly from low self-esteem and poor motivation.	Boys seem less willing to struggle to overcome difficulties in understanding their work. Boys are less likely to work consistently hard than girls and are more easily distracted. In areas such as coursework, boys find it more difficult to organise their time effectively.
Girls are more willing to do homework and spend more time on it.	Girls give more thought to their futures and to the importance of qualifications in achievement of this, whereas boys do not seem as concerned.
Moir and Moir claim schools have become too 'girl friendly'.	Boys are now forced to learn in ways that do not suit them. This may include an emphasis on verbal skills and non-competitive environments.
Orly Katz says that peer pressure, the fear of ridicule and the need to fit in, all contribute to boys not being seen to 'try'.	Low self-esteem in boys may be linked to images of incompetent men found in advertising, sitcoms and soaps, etc. This low self-esteem may also be linked to the decline in traditional male jobs, leaving boys uncertain about their futures and lacking motivation.

Inside school factors	Outside school factors
Teacher/pupil interactions	Socialisation
Curriculum being gendered	Job market/changing job opportunities
Introduction of the National Curriculum	
Hidden curriculum	Decline in manufacturing sector and crisis of masculinity
Resources	Law/legal changes
Homework/coursework	Feminist movement
Role models/feminisation of teaching	
Government initiatives	Girls' priorities
Single-sex schooling	Equal opportunities policies
Boys more likely to form anti-school subcultures (Paul Willis)	Family changes – more dual-earner households
Girls receive less attention in the classroom and boys dominate classroom discussions (Michelle Stanworth)	Differential parental encouragement
Boys dominate equipment in practical subjects such as PE and Science	Girls are more likely to spend time at home revising whereas boys are more likely to spend time playing sports (Angela McRobbie)

Support for the argument that gender affects educational achievement is:

In the 1980s boys used to outperform girls. Today girls achieve better than boys at both GCSE and A Level. Girls do better by about 8 points at GCSE.

In 2015–2016 across all ethnic groups, girls were more likely to achieve A* to C in English and Maths GCSE than boys – 67 per cent of girls did so, compared to 59 per cent of boys

There are about 30 per cent more girls than boys at university but males tend to achieve higher than females at university. More males get first class degrees and PHDs.

Girls achieve better GCSE and A Level results than boys.

Evidence against the argument that gender affects educational achievement is:

Many of the studies used are outdated. Teacher training is now better in terms of an awareness of gender inequality and the curriculum and resources are a lot more balanced.

Some of the studies are from unrepresentative samples. Stanworth's study only used one school and therefore we cannot draw generalisations from this.

There are many policies designed to increase the number of females taking STEM subjects.

A 2007 DfES report 2007 stated 'Analysis of the attainment data shows that other factors or a combination of factors, such as ethnicity and social class, have a greater bearing on educational achievement than gender considered on its own'.

It is a myth that boys prefer male teachers. A number of studies have found that while there are more female teachers than male teachers, most pupils prioritise the teacher's ability and how caring they are rather than their gender.

Boys may prefer to spend their leisure time playing sports whereas girls may spend their time reading or communicating with their friends. Does this affect their educational achievement?

Think link
Although this revision spread is about gender and educational achievement, try to also think of ways of bringing in feminist theories of education.

REVISION BOOSTER

Research by the Department of Education published in February 2019 shows that 59 per cent of boys said that a STEM subject was their favourite lesson compared to just 32 per cent of girls. Nick Gibb, the schools minister, wishes to change the attitudes of girls towards these subjects so that more females can take up careers in engineering, construction and manufacturing.

Key figure

Melissa Tarris, a professor at Edinburgh University says that 'there are hardly any women with expertise being shown to children'. A recent study found that only 29 out of 328 academics in children's storybooks are female. 25 of professors and 45 per cent of academic staff at UK universities are female yet only 9 per cent of academics in children's storybooks are female. When she was made a professor her own son said that she couldn't be a professor as she isn't a man. Tarris believes that book publishers should be challenging gender stereotypes.

Knowledge check

1. Describe what is meant by 'feminisation of education'.
   (2 marks)

2. Outline how schools may socialise children into their gender roles. **(5 marks)**

3. Choose one inside school factor and outline how it may explain why girls do better than boys. **(5 marks)**

4. Outline why girls may be less likely than boys to choose STEM subjects. **(5 marks)**

Spec spotlight

3.4 Factors affecting educational achievement: types of school

Link to textbook

pp 110–111: Different types of school

pp 112–113: Parental choice and competition between schools

AO2 Apply

Look at the graph showing progress scores for reading, writing and maths for different school types found at https://www.telegraph. co.uk/education/0/academies-pros-cons/.. What can you learn about the educational achievement of pupils in reading, writing and maths in different schools?

Take it further

Look at the graph showing average point score per entry for A Level students by institution type, England 2018, found at

https://assets.publishing.service. gov.uk/government/uploads/ system/uploads/attachment_data/ file/772074/2018_provisional_A_ level_and_other16-18_results_in_ England_-_update.pdf (page 13).

Which type of schools performed better at A Level in 2018? What are some of the sociological reasons to explain this?

REVISION BOOSTER

In 2016, research indicated that single-sex schooling works for girls as girls who attend these schools perform better than those in mixed schools. Even when other factors such as social class are taken into account, girls who are taught separately still achieve higher grades. Reasons suggested for this include that girls learn in a different way from boys and there is no detrimental gender stereotyping so girls can be more confident in themselves.

5–16 education in the UK

All children aged between 5 and 16 years in the UK are entitled to a free education.

The most common types of schools are community schools, comprehensive schools, academies and grammar schools. Studies show that some types of school give children an advantage in terms of their educational achievement. The government in the UK has tried to offer parents more choice in the type of school they decide to send their child to. This has led to a variety of different types of schools in the UK.

Does the type of school a pupil attends have an effect on their educational achievement?

Types of school

Independent schools	These schools are not run or paid for by the government. Parents pay money to schools that are run as businesses.
Comprehensive schools	These are non-selective, state-funded schools under the control of government. They are not influenced by religious or business groups. They tend to be quite large.
Grammar schools	These are state-funded schools, but select most of their pupils based on academic ability. There is often an exam to get in.
Faith schools	These are schools run by a particular religion rather than by the government. They have to follow the national curriculum but can choose what to teach in religious education.
Academies	These are state schools which get their funding directly from the government rather than their local council. They are run by individual charitable bodies called academy trusts. They are independent from the local council.
Free schools	They are a type of academy; a non-profit-making, state-funded school which is free to attend. They are not controlled by a Local Authority (LA) but instead governed by a non-profit, charitable trust.

AO3
Evaluation

School type	Advantages	Disadvantages
Independent	• Usually get much higher results than state schools. More than twice as likely to get an A* at A Level. Pupils are more likely to attend prestigious universities such as Oxford or Cambridge. 7 per cent of UK pupils attend private schools yet make up 45 per cent of Oxbridge students. • These schools normally have smaller class sizes – pupils can get more time and attention from the teacher. • Higher results are also helped by an academic culture, better facilities and extracurricular activities and better discipline.	• Students may have to travel a long distance to attend or even board there. They can put pupils under a lot of pressure to perform well academically. • They are usually only available to middle-class pupils due to the high cost of the school fees. It is estimated that it costs, on average, £286,000 for 14 years of private education. They help to reproduce social inequality. • May not cater for less-able or SEND pupils.

School type	Advantages	Disadvantages
Comprehensive	• Caters for children of all abilities and backgrounds – equal opportunities. Attempts to break social barriers. • Can have better resources and facilities due to the amount of funding they receive. They have high numbers of pupils joining the school therefore they receive higher amounts of funding. Larger schools are cheaper to run on a per pupil basis. • No entrance exam, so not a barrier to social equality.	• Large intake so teachers may not get to know pupils individually. • Continuation of setting and streaming is a disadvantage as lower-class pupils are often in the lower sets and research suggests that they do not receive the same quality of teaching as pupils in the higher sets. • Offer parents a limited choice. Catchment areas aren't free of class division.
Grammar	• More-able students are challenged in a higher-achieving environment. • They give opportunity for able pupils from lower income families to succeed and achieve a high standard of education – improved social mobility. • Tend to get excellent academic results. As it is a more academic environment, more-able pupils are less likely to be bullied for wanting to work hard.	• Acts to the advantage of middle-class parents and pupils. • Wealthier children have a better chance of getting in as their parents can afford to pay for private tuition and other materials to help pass the entrance exam. • Reinforces social division as the majority of pupils who attend them are middle class. The Sutton Trust found that only 3 per cent of the pupils at grammar schools receive free school meals.
Faith	• Generally achieve above average results. • Receive a religious education supporting their own religious belief. • Some parents prefer the religious ethos and teaching in a faith school. They give pupils a strong sense of identity.	• May exclude certain groups of people and reinforce community isolation. Can create a segregated society. Can be divisive. • The intake of a faith school is not fully representative of the local area. Some may discriminate in their employment or promotion of staff. • Acts to the advantage of middle-class parents who know how to 'work the system' and may rent near a school or attend church purely in order to meet admissions criteria.
Academies	• Academy status brings autonomy. Freedom from the constraints of the National Curriculum. • Aim to fill the gaps in areas where there are not enough school places for children. The freedom over the budget means more control over where money is assigned in the school. • Aim to boost struggling schools in deprived inner-city areas. Receive more funding per pupil than state comprehensive pupils.	• Some teachers and parents see this as a move towards privatisation of the education system. • They can be seen as damaging to existing schools around them. • Some people claim it gives free rein to religious sponsors to teach topics such as creationism over biology. • Concern has been raised over staff salaries. The directors of several academy trusts were found to be earning more than some of the UK's best-paid university vice-chancellors. • They can employ untrained staff. • Typically have fewer children who receive free school meals.
Free	• They receive more funding per pupil than state comprehensive pupils and have freedom from the constraints of the National Curriculum. • Some people argue that they raise standards in all schools, in part by creating more local competition. • Allow parents to have more choice in the type of school their child attends.	• Angela Rayner MP, Labour's Shadow Secretary of State for Education, claims that they 'neither improve standards, nor empower staff or parents'. • Teachers do not have to be qualified. • They divert money away from existing schools in the community, but typically have fewer children who receive free school meals. • They have led to a surplus of school places – many open with only 60 per cent of the school places filled.

Think link

Although this revision spread is about the types of school in the UK today, try to also think of ways of bringing in some of the theories of education. For example, what might a functionalist or a Marxist believe about each different school and why?

Knowledge check

1. Describe what is meant by an independent school. **(2 marks)**
2. Name and describe two different types of school in the UK today. **(4 marks)**
3. Describe one type of school that pupils aged 11–16 might attend and explain the advantages of this type of school. **(5 marks)**

Spec spotlight

3.1 Sociological theories of the role of education: functionalist theory of education, Marxist theory of education serving the needs of capitalism, feminist theory of education

Link to textbook

pp 114–115: The functionalist view of education
pp 116–117: The Marxist view of education
pp 118–119: The feminist view of education

AO2 Apply

Research and write down the reasons why Bowles and Gintis say there is a link between school and the workplace. What specific examples from the school day and workplace would support these points? Think about the school day and how it is organised, how pupils are motivated and rewarded, the hierarchy within the school, competition and meritocracy.

Take it further

Look at Sir Ken Robinson's TED Talk about schools killing creativity (https://www.ted.com/talks/ken_robinson_says_schools_kill_creativity) – how can you link this to Marxism and the role of education?

Sir Ken Robinson believes that schools kill creativity. Listen to his TED Talk to find out why he believes this.

The role of education

According to Talcott Parsons, a functionalist, education has three functions.	1. Teach skills required for work. 2. Allocation of correct people for appropriate job/form of social selection. 3. Agency of secondary socialisation/helps to socialise children into the values of society/creating a shared culture.
	Emphasises meritocracy so there are no unfair inequalities. Helps create social order. The education system is beneficial to society as a whole.
Marxists also believe education has three functions.	1. Teaches skills required for work and prepares them for the world of work in a capitalist society. 2. Justifies inequality. 3. Passes on ruling-class ideology that supports capitalism.
	Education serves the interests of the ruling class/bourgeoisie. Education produces obedient workers to support the economic system.
Feminists believe the education system is patriarchal and reinforces gender roles and norms.	Education is about reproducing patriarchy. Men dominate the top positions in school – head teacher, etc.
	There is a moral panic about boys' underachievement – this focus reflects a patriarchal and male-dominated society. Subject choices tend to be gendered.

Who are the key figures?

The functionalist Emile Durkheim says that education passes on norms and values in order to integrate people into society.	For Durkheim, school is a smaller version of society where children learn to interact with the other members. Their experience at school prepares them for the roles they will play in adulthood and in the workplace.
Functionalist Parsons says that education is the bridge between the family and the wider world.	Parsons also says that education sorts people into their suitable and appropriate roles.
Marxist Louis Althusser believes that education socialises working-class children into accepting their lower status than the middle class. Marxist sociologists Sam Bowles and Herb Gintis say there is a link between school and work.	Pupils are taught to accept hierarchy at school – work also has a hierarchy. Pupils are motivated by grades to do boring work – workers rewarded with pay to do boring work. School day broken into units – so is school work. At school and work, subservience (following the rules) is rewarded.
Spender	Spender says teachers give boys and girls different types of attention. Girls are generally praised for appearance, good behaviour and neat work.
Anne Colley	Anne Colley found gender differences in subject choice despite the introduction of the National Curriculum. She found that girls tend to prefer art and drama, and boys tend to prefer PE and ICT.
A. Stables and F. Wikeley	Stables and Wikeley further support Colley's research as they have also found evidence of gender differences in subject choices. Boys preferred PE, technology and science whereas girls preferred art, English and drama.

Strengths and weaknesses of the functionalist perspective are:

Functionalists focus on the positives of the education system.

Education is not meritocratic – evidenced by differences in class, gender and ethnicity and achievement.

Who you know is still more important than what you know in some parts of society.

Marxists argue that functionalists ignore the negative side of the education system. They criticise functionalists like Durkheim for assuming that norms and values promoted in school are those of society as a whole.

Functionalists ignore the negative side of education, for example, bullying.

Strengths and weaknesses of the Marxist perspective are:

Marxism helps to explain why there is inequality in society.

Paul Willis says that education doesn't turn out an obedient workforce. This is evidenced by the existence of an anti-school subculture.

It can ignore other effects, like that of gender and can assume people are passive victims.

It has been suggested that Marxists over-exaggerate the link between school and the workplace.

What do Marxists believe about the role of the education system?

Strengths and weaknesses of the feminist perspective are:

Despite improvements in girls' education, many are still not breaking the glass ceiling.

Some feminists argue that traditional gender roles are still reinforced in school through the sports played in PE, for example.

However, a focus on gender ignores the effects of class and ethnicity.

Does education help women to break through the glass ceiling?

Spec spotlight

5.1 Sociological theories of stratification: conflict versus consensus debate on stratification, consensus view of functionalism, conflict views of Marxism, Weber and feminism

Link to textbook

pp 126–127: Functionalist views on stratification

pp 128–129: Marxist views on stratification

pp 130–131: Weber: What did he say about stratification?

pp 132–133: Feminist views on stratification

What do you notice about the social class pyramid?

AO2 Apply

What do you think would happen in the UK if all jobs paid equal wages? Some jobs at the moment get high rates of pay compared to others – professional footballers, surgeons, lawyers and so on. Even teachers can earn above the average wage for the UK! Could the system work? What would be good about it? Not so good about it?

Consensus view

Stratification is a way of seeing the different inequalities in society as different layers, like those in a trifle.	The consensus view is the view of functionalists. They compare the way a society works to the way a human body works. All of the different parts of society play a role (function) in keeping society working.
In the consensus view all societies have some kind of inequality.	Just as the heart and the brain play a part in keeping a body healthy so do different parts of society. Inequality plays a key role in making society work and keeping society healthy.
K. Davis and W.E. Moore were key functionalist thinkers.	Having unequal rewards is positive for society as it motivates people to aim for the best and most important jobs. The fear of poverty or failure also motivates people to work hard.
Inequality is fair and necessary.	Davis and Moore called matching people to the right jobs 'role allocation'. Without it society cannot expect to get the best people for key jobs, such as CEO, doctor or prime minister.

Conflict view

Conflict views see inequality as unfair and not all will agree.	There are three main conflict views: Marxism, feminism and the views of Max Weber.
Marxism sees our society as being unfair and based on a conflict between ruling class and working class.	Marxists believe that societies have always been based on inequality. The most important inequality in capitalism is class inequality. The ruling class exploit the working class, making a profit out of their misery. Marx thought that this system would collapse.
Feminists see the most important inequality as that between men and women.	Feminists, like Ann Oakley and Sylvia Walby, argue that society is male dominated. They call this 'domination patriarchy'. Feminists are concerned about inequalities in pay, power, life-chances and exploitation by men.
One of the key debates in this part of the syllabus is about whether inequality is fair and essential for society.	The main debate is between functionalists who believe that inequality is needed in society and the conflict theorists. Marxists, in particular, believe that there could be a fairer society without inequality. Feminists would also say that inequality between men and women could be reduced.

Key figure

Max Weber had a different view of stratification which was still a conflict view. He thought that a person's social class, based on their job, was an important part of inequality. However, he also thought that the groups people belonged to and their market position (the amount of money they are able to earn) affected their position in the stratification system.

Strengths of the consensus (functionalist) view are:

Inequality is needed as no one would want to do the stressful jobs which need a lot of training, such as a doctor.

Countries that have tried communism, such as Russia and East Germany, have not succeeded. Some groups have still had power and privilege. Most people were very poor. This proves inequality is necessary.

Davis and Moore argue that people are born with different levels of ability. Unequal rewards help match the right person to the right job.

Weaknesses of the functionalist view are:

Inequality is becoming even greater in the UK since the financial crisis of 2008. Do the mega rich really need such huge rewards?

Marxists argue that capitalism makes inequality necessary because it socialises us to be greedy and need big rewards.

An article in the *Economist* from June 2018 which showed tax data suggested that the top 1 per cent of earners get up to a tenth of total household income, a higher proportion than in previous decades. This has increased in the last ten years. Does there need to be this much inequality?

Strengths of the conflict (Marxist) view are:

Ideas like the 'old boys' network' show how inequality is unfair and not good for society. The best people do not always get the best jobs. Connections and influence always help.

There is a lot of evidence to suggest that the UK is becoming more unequal especially since the 2008 financial crisis. In April 2018, *The Independent* reported food bank use to be higher than ever.

Even if Marxist-style communism does not work, Marxists ask important questions about capitalism in the UK. Does there need to be such a great deal of inequality?

Weaknesses of the conflict (Marxist) view are:

Communism has failed almost everywhere it has been tried. Even places like Cuba and Vietnam, where it has continued, have struggled at times.

Society might collapse without inequality. No one would do the most difficult jobs.

Peter Saunders, a New Right sociologist, says that the best way to organise society is to have unequal rewards. The middle class do get the best jobs, and this is because they inherit the best talent, hard work and intelligence from their parents.

Strengths of the conflict (feminist) view are:

They have improved the life-chances of women, e.g. Equal Pay Act 1970.

Improving the life-chances of women is good for society as not using their abilities is a waste of talent.

They have exposed the way that women have been mistreated and exploited in the nuclear family.

Weaknesses of the conflict (feminist) view are:

Changes making women more equal have had an impact on men called the 'crisis of masculinity'.

The New Right argue that women working long hours would be bad for their children and bad for society.

The New Right and functionalists argue that women are naturally more suited to housework and childcare because of their nature.

How much inequality is necessary for society?

Think link
How do the theories link to media, health, education and crime? These theories spread across all topics.

Knowledge check

1. Describe what is meant by 'stratification'.   (2 marks)
2. Outline the functionalist view on stratification.   (4 marks)
3. Explain two reasons why feminists say that women are not equal in society.   (4 marks)
4. Discuss whether inequality is necessary for society.   (9 marks)

Spec spotlight

5.2 Different forms and sources of power and authority

5.4 Factors which may influence access to life-chances and power

Link to textbook

pp 136–137: What is power?
pp 138–139: What is authority?

What would a Marxist say about power and authority in relation to the picture ? What would a Feminist say about power and authority in relation to the picture?

AO2 Apply

Explain, using Weber's ideas, why the following people have authority:

- *Teacher*
- *Donald Trump*
- *The Pope*
- *England football team manager*
- *Doctor*
- *Alan Sugar*
- *Mayor*
- *Chief of a Native American tribe*
- *Captain America.*

Take it further

What would a Marxist or feminist say about the sources of power of each of these. Try to use sociological language to do this.

Power

Power is about the ability of individuals and/or groups to influence decisions about themselves and other people.	Individuals do not always think of how much power they have in everyday life. This is closely linked to the life-chances of individuals. Life-chances include the chance of getting your choice of job, house or area you live in, proving your innocence in a court case or getting the hospital treatment you need.
There are informal and formal sources of power.	Power is exercised through the use of sanctions by those in positions of power. Sanctions may include rewards and punishments. Those in positions of power may be able to shape decisions they want.
Informal sources of power include the family, schools, religion and workplaces.	There are differences in power among even informal sources of power. Some members of a peer group may have greater informal power than others.
Formal sources of power include agencies of social control, such as the police, courts and army.	Functionalists would see the formal sources of power as necessary to keep social order. Marxists would see the formal sources of power as favouring the ruling class.

Authority

Authority is about having the power and the right to make decisions.	People with authority are viewed as having the right to make decisions. In the UK, local councils and parliament are voted into power and are given the right to use power to make decisions.
Different groups vary in their access to positions of authority.	Age, gender, class and ethnicity all affect the chances of someone being put into positions of authority. This can affect life-chances.
Functionalists would see authority as playing a positive role. It enables decisions to be made by leaders to benefit society.	Functionalists would see individuals as having some access to power through democracy. They vote to put people into positions of authority. This benefits society and is the best way to run society.
Max Weber has one of the most important theories of why people accept authority.	Weber argued that there were three main sources of authority. Traditional authority is based on custom. Rational–legal authority is based on clear and logical rules for decision making, such as a democratic election. Charismatic authority is based on the personality of the leader.

Strengths of the feminist view of power and authority are:

Feminists explain how men are able to be dominant in society.	Feminists explain how society is patriarchal and woman are not equal. Four times as many men as women in Britain earn over £100,000. This shows the lack of women in higher positions of authority.	Feminists have helped to gain more power for women. The Harvey Weinstein case shows that women felt they had the power to come forward and report the way that he and other men had abused their power.

Weaknesses of the feminist view of power and authority are:

Men have less power than women in some aspects of family life, including custody battles of children.	Functionalists, such as Talcott Parsons, would see traditional gender roles with males in charge as good for society.	Women's push for positions of power and authority results in children in nurseries and day care. The New Right sees this as bad for society.

Strengths of the conflict (Marxist) view of power and authority are:

It shows the great inequalities of power between social classes. Some groups are excluded from society.	Marxism shows how higher social classes are 'helped' to get what they want through things like the old boys' network.	Marxism shows how the higher classes have the power to gain positions of power. For example, 19 out of 54 British prime ministers since 1721 have attended Eton, the famous public school for the privileged.

Weaknesses of the conflict (Marxist) view of power and authority are:

Social class may not be as important as in the past.	It ignores gender differences in power.	The New Right says that the higher social classes are in power because they have more ability and make more effort.

Strengths of Weber's view of the source of authority are:

Weber's three sources of authority can explain authority throughout human history from the ancient Egyptians and Romans to today.	Weber's view can explain and justify why people have the authority to use power.	Weber's view explains how rational–legal authority is a more modern and fairer way of organising society.

Weaknesses of Weber's view of the source of authority are:

Some leaders have aspects of more than one source of authority, e.g. Hitler.	Feminists would criticise Weber's ideas for failing to explain the lack of female authority in society, i.e. the glass ceiling.	Marxists would criticise Weber's view as it does not consider the influence of wealth and the power of the ruling class.

Rational–legal authority tends to be seen as the modern way of deciding who is in power and what decisions get made? How were things decided in the past? Think about how leaders were chosen and decisions made in medieval times. How was the king chosen?

Key figure

Steven Lukes was influenced by Marxism. He said that power had three parts to it. These are:
- the power to make decisions, e.g. what to do about pollution
- the power to control whether an issue is even discussed, e.g. whether pollution is even an issue
- the power to control what people want and think. Powerful groups, like men and the ruling class are able to shape what people think through control of the media and advertising. e.g. if people do not hear about pollution they are not worried about it.

Think link

Try to make links between topics. How might the topic of power relate to crime? You might consider the role of the courts and police.

Knowledge check

1. Identify two different sources of authority. **(2 marks)**
2. Outline two different sources of power. **(4 marks)**
3. Explain why some individuals have greater authority than others. **(4 marks)**
4. Discuss the importance of differences in power in society. **(9 marks)**

Spec spotlight

5.3 Equality/inequality in relation to class

5.4 Factors which may influence access to life-chances and power: with specific reference to social class, private schooling, old boys' network, affluent worker including the work of Devine

Link to textbook

pp 140–141: Do we live in a classless society?

pp 142–143: Are inequalities of social class still important in the UK?

pp 144–145: How does social class affect life-chances?

Many traditional working-class jobs have disappeared. There are now new jobs which are non-manual but low in pay and status. Can you think of any others?

AO2 Apply

Take the strengths and weaknesses of Fiona Devine's study and write sentences about them using the following words: dated, typical, representativeness, validity, detailed, reliability, sample.

Take it further

Explain why Devine deliberately chose a non-representative sample.

Class, life-chances and inequality

An individual's social class is normally decided by their occupation. In the UK there are traditionally three main social classes: working, middle and upper class.

The working class were traditionally a large group made up of people who worked in lower-paid and manual jobs. The middle classes worked in non-manual jobs and had higher aspirations. The upper classes were a smaller group consisting of those with power, wealth and privilege.

Social class is an important part of sociological study.

Since the 1970s, gender, ethnicity and other social differences have become more important in sociology. Marxists only see two important classes in society. These are the ruling class (bourgeoisie) and the working class (proletariat). Marxists believe that class still has the strongest effect on life-chances.

Social class is shown statistically to have a great effect on life-chances in many aspects of life including education, health, wealth and crime.

A study set up by Conservative MP Justine Greening in 2018 found that half of UK workers believe a regional accent and a working-class background are barriers to success.

Greening, the former education secretary, said that the study showed that people think there is a 'class ceiling'. Personal connections helped to get the best jobs. This suits the middle class better than working-class people.

Some sociologists, such as the New Right, argue that social class is no longer important in the UK. They believe that we now live in a classless society.

Many traditional working-class jobs have disappeared in the UK. New Right sociologists, such as Peter Saunders and Charles Murray argue that the reason for some working-class people having worse life-chances is down to poor attitudes. Those who have the ability and want to get on can do so.

Research and social class

A Sky News report in February 2018 based on data from the Office for National Statistics showed that the top 10 per cent in the UK had as much wealth as the bottom half.

This sounds quite a big difference, but the Equality Trust, as reported on BBC Bitesize, showed that the 100 wealthiest people in the UK have as much wealth as the poorest 18 million. The figures can be looked at in different ways but the overall picture of inequality in the UK is of large differences.

Pierre Bourdieu argued that higher social classes had an advantage through cultural capital.

Cultural capital refers to the values and attitudes that enable parents of the higher social classes to help their children to be successful. Higher social classes are likely to have connections and privilege. Private education can help this to happen. Working-class parents cannot afford this advantage.

John Goldthorpe and David Lockwood carried out the affluent worker study in Luton car factories in 1961–62.

Goldthorpe and Lockwood set out to try to prove whether social class was disappearing. Would the affluent workers become like the middle class? They found that the working class was changing but was not disappearing.

Fiona Devine repeated this study in the 1980s.

Fiona Devine found a sense of working-class identity still existing in her study. Her study showed that we are not living in a classless society.

Strengths of the argument that Britain is now a classless society are:

There are fewer manual jobs than in the past. Shipbuilding, mining and steel work have been in decline in the UK.

The minimum wage helps everyone get a good wage.

The percentage of young people going to university has increased from 3.4 per cent in 1950, to 8.4 per cent in 1970, 19.3 per cent in 1990 and 33 per cent in 2000. In 2017 the figure was almost half.

Trade union membership is falling in the UK. Being part of a trade union was part of working-class identity.

Postmodernist sociologists argue that social class is disappearing. People no longer have a job for life. People get their identity from the products they buy and their social media identity, which they create themselves.

Weaknesses of the argument that Britain is now a classless society are:

The government is very concerned about the disadvantages in education faced by poorer children.

A report published by NHS England in March 2018 showed that life expectancy and mental health problems are still strongly affected by deprivation. Working-class people are most likely to be deprived.

Positions of power in government are still dominated by those who are privately educated. 29 per cent of the 2017 MPs elected went to private school. This is four times greater than that of the population as a whole, although this is an improvement from previous elections. In 1983, 51 per cent of MPs were privately educated and that figure was 35 per cent in 2010.

Strengths of the argument that social class does not affect life-chances and power are:

MPs in parliament in 2017 were less 'posh' than ever. There were over 51 per cent who went to comprehensive schools.

Access to health care and education is available to all in the UK. Loans for university fees do not have to be paid back unless students earn wages over £21,000 a year, which is close to the national average wage of £25,000. Numbers attending university are up.

There are many examples of successful people who have worked their way up from poor backgrounds, such as Alan Sugar.

Weaknesses of the argument that social class does not affect life-chances and power are:

Working-class people are more likely to be victims of crime and more likely to be in prison.

Working-class people are more likely to be working in the 'gig' economy or on zero hours contracts. As such they have no job security, fewer rights and are not entitled to holiday pay or redundancy.

Working-class people are stereotyped in the media. Most of the characters in soaps like Coronation Street and EastEnders are working class and are often linked to crime. This may lead to prejudice and discrimination.

What advantages does the upper class have in the UK?

Think link
The education system is one of the clearest ways that the class system can be seen. What advantages do children who go to private schools have? Link the information from the education topic to this.

REVISION BOOSTER

The 'Does class still exist?' debate is a complex one. You may have to answer a 9-mark question like this. Create coloured cards for for and against the disappearance of class. Practice your introduction to the question:

Does class still exist?

Key figure

Basil Bernstein wrote *Elaborated and Restricted Code* (1971) which studied the differences in the ways middle-class and working-class children speak. He found that working-class children found it hard to understand the 'posh' talk used by teachers, which he called 'elaborated code'. He called the local accents and slang used by working-class children 'restricted code'.

Some sociologists have developed his ideas to claim that working-class language is inferior. Others, such as **William Labov**, argue that working-class speech is just different, neither better or worse than middle-class. Whether this is true or not, working-class children may be at a disadvantage in school.

Which code do you speak? Can you speak both?

Knowledge check

1. Outline what is meant by 'social class'. **(2 marks)**

2. Identify two ways that social class can affect life-chances. **(4 marks)**

3. Explain why some sociologists say that social class is no longer important. **(4 marks)**

4. 'Working-class people have different life-chances compared to others.' Do you agree? **(9 marks)**

Spec spotlight

5.3 Equality/inequality in relation to gender

5.4 Factors which may influence access to life-chances and power: social construction of identity/roles, stereotyping, media representation; with specific reference to gender, sexism, glass ceiling, patriarchy, including the work of Walby, crisis of masculinity

Link to textbook

AO2 Apply

Maria is a married woman with two children. Her husband has a good job and is very tired when he gets home. She got some of the best GCSE and A Level results in her school and studied law at university gaining an honours degree.

Maria has a job at a law firm and is seen as a reliable employee, although she finds her life very busy and does not know how she fits it all in. She is frustrated as she has been promoted to supervisor but wants to be on the management team. Maria has tried to gain promotion but keeps missing out. The firm recently appointed a man to the management team who is less well qualified than her and has only just joined the company.

Explain why this is happening using sociological words such as prejudice, sexism, stereotyping, discrimination.

Take it further

Continue the work you did for the activity above, now using more words to bring in other sociological ideas. Add an opposing argument using sociological theories or ideas.

Gender socialisation and inequality

Feminists argue that traditional gender roles are harmful to both males and females.

Girls and boys are traditionally socialised to follow different sets of norms and values, which we call masculinity and femininity. Feminists argue that socialisation limits the opportunities open to both genders and affects life-chances. Women are particularly affected by this as society is patriarchal or male dominated.

Some sociologists talk about a 'gender quake' which has changed the way that people are socialised and the balance of power in society.

Some sociologists argue that the media have begun to represent males and females in more equal ways with less stereotyping. Schools now offer equal choices for girls and boys; girls are encouraged to pursue non-traditionally female careers in science and engineering.

Legislation has been passed which has aimed to improve the life-chances of women. Feminist ideas have helped to bring about these changes.

Many laws have been passed promoting more equal opportunities for women. The Equal Pay Act 1970 was very important. The Sex Discrimination Act 1975 protected men and women from discrimination due to sex or marital status. Although these laws have been supported by further laws, such as the Equality Act 2010, feminists would question how successful they have been.

Changes in women's gender roles have had an impact upon men also. The uncertainty faced by men about their position has been called the 'crisis of masculinity' by sociologists.

The crisis of masculinity has been caused by the changes in men's position. This is partly because their role has changed as women have become more independent. Men's traditional roles as head of the family and main breadwinner have been challenged. In addition, changes to the nature of work mean that there are fewer 'real men's jobs' which involve strength and physical labour. Some men have found these changes difficult.

Evidence of gender inequality and life-chances

Women are more likely to be living as a lone-parent family. This number had grown since the early 1970s and has remained high since. There were 1.6 million female lone-parent families in 2017 compared to 179,000 male.

Despite this, the Joseph Rowntree Foundation revealed that in 2018 having children increased women's chances of living in poverty. 5.2 million women lived in poverty compared to 4.7 million men.

The family still may not be equal due to the idea of the dual burden or the triple shift.

The gender pay gap has shrunk from 17.4 per cent in 1997 to 9.4 per cent in 2017, according to the Office for National Statistics.

Despite this, the gender pay gap will still take decades to close. Despite the fact that the law was passed in 1970, women are still waiting for true equality.

The glass ceiling was still very much in evidence in 2018. Only a quarter of the directors of the 250 top firms in the UK are female, according to Consultancy.uk.

Girls have outperformed boys at every level of education since the 1990s.

Despite this, males still dominate the top jobs and there is still a gender pay gap. Jobs are still seen as gendered and jobs linked to traditional female roles, such as nursing and child care, are still low paid. Women may face sexism, harassment and discrimination based on stereotypes still found in the media.

Men's life-chances do not compare favourably to women's in some areas. For instance, lower life expectancy, higher suicide rates and more likely to be a victim of crime or be in prison.

The representation of men in the media has also changed and there are pressures on men to be physically fit or have a 'six-pack'. On the positive side, men may feel comfortable to express their masculinity in a variety of ways, according to Bob Connell, an Australian sociologist.

Men still enjoy better pay, status and power on the whole than women. However, the decline in men's performance in education is having an impact on the life-chances of working-class boys, in particular.

Strengths of the argument that women's life-chances and power have improved are:

We now have a second female prime minister. The proportion of female MPs elected in the 2017 election was 32 per cent, the highest ever.

Power in families is more equally shared. Wilmott and Young's symmetrical families are now seen as a social norm.

Girls are socialised differently now. The labelling that happened in the 1970s is much less common now and equal opportunities have increased.

Weaknesses of the argument that women's life-chances and power have improved are:

Sexist stereotyping is still common in the media. Women are still shown in traditional roles or as objects of beauty. Feminists argue that this idea controls women's behaviour.

The evidence of the glass ceiling and the gender pay gap is a major weakness in this argument. Women are more likely to live in poverty, less likely to have a high income, be wealthy or have power over their lives.

Patriarchy still traps women in domestic roles. The double burden increases the expectations of women to go out to work and still be the domestic goddess.

Strengths of the argument that men's life-chances and power are declining are:

Men have worse life-chances in many ways including many aspects of health.

Men are less likely to gain custody of their children after a relationship break up. From their role as head of the family, men are now in a weaker position.

Traditional male characteristics, such as aggression and physical strength are not seen as useful any more.

Weaknesses of the argument that men's life-chances and power are declining are:

Mentalhealth.org.uk says that women in England are more likely than men to have a common mental health problem and are almost twice as likely to be diagnosed with anxiety disorders.

Men are still getting the best jobs and earning higher wages. The old boys' network still helps men achieve.

Women going out to work has not helped either gender. Family life has suffered as both man and woman need to work to maintain the standard of living needed.

Write a caption for this picture. Include sociological language.

REVISION BOOSTER

On the evaluation questions (worth 9 marks on this topic), avoid using subjective language, e.g. 'I think that'. Try to use neutral language so that you sound as if your essay is almost like a scientific report, e.g. 'The evidence/arguments so far would suggest that…'

Key figure

Sylvia Walby, a British sociologist argued that women are disadvantaged in a number of ways.
- The family, schools and the media are sexist and patriarchal. They cause inequality for women.
- Men believe the stereotypes of women and discriminate against them, not giving them the best jobs or paying them fairly.
- Men exploit women's unpaid work at home.

Think link

How could you use the concept of the chivalry thesis to answer questions about gender and life-chances?

Knowledge check

1. Outline what is meant by 'gender'. **(2 marks)**
2. Identify two ways that prejudice can affect life-chances. **(4 marks)**
3. Explain why some sociologists say that there is a crisis of masculinity. **(4 marks)**
4. 'The life-chances of women are improving.' Do you agree? **(9 marks)**

Spec spotlight

5.3 Equality/inequality in relation to age

5.4 Factors which may influence access to life-chances and power: social construction of identity/roles/status, prejudice, discrimination, stereotyping, labelling, media representation, moral panics; with specific reference to age, ageism

Link to textbook

pp 154–155: How do the norms of different age groups vary in different societies?

pp 156–157: How does the media present different age groups?

pp 158–159: How does age affect life-chances?

AO2 Apply

A 2017 survey of 1400 workers found that over half of under 18s feel they're not taken seriously at work, and three-quarters of 25- to 34-year-olds consider themselves having failed to get jobs or treated differently because they are 'too young'. Over half of over 55s also said they had been treated unfavourably.

Adapted from *The Independent*, December 2017

What explanations could you suggest for the report? Use sociological language from the spec spotlight to strengthen your argument.

How might ageism affect these interviews?

Take it further

How could society reduce ageism? What strategies could the government introduce?

Age in the UK

Age is socially constructed. Our ideas of what to expect from different age groups change over time.	Philippe Aries showed that the idea of childhood as a special protected time did not become common until Victorian times.
	Laws have been put in place to protect children and children have less freedom in some ways than in the past. However, children have access to different dangers through the Internet.
Youth has often been seen as a problem by the older generation.	The sociological idea of 'teenagers' appeared in the USA in the 1950s at the time of rock and roll. Manufacturers saw a chance to sell lots of products to teenagers. At the same time however, there has been a series of moral panics about youth. In 2018 the recorded increase in knife crime was a source of much media attention. Young people suffer prejudice as a result of the stereotypes spread by this attention.
The increase in life expectancy and lower birth rate mean that the UK has an ageing population with growing numbers of elderly people.	The older generation run the risk of being seen as an increased burden on society. Retired people are seen as taking money from the state and also require lots of support from the NHS and social care. A smaller number of under 50s must support them. As a result of some of these concerns, the retirement age has been pushed up to 67 years.
	The older generation are seen to have had better life-chances in some ways as many of them own property. Rising house prices make it more difficult for under 40s to buy property.
Ageism has been recognised in the UK as unfair and not good for society. Legislation has been passed to protect people against ageism.	The 2010 Equality Act made it illegal to discriminate or harass people on the grounds of age. The Royal Society for Public Health published a study in 2018 which showed how harmful stereotypes of old age can be on people's health and well-being. It found that ageism was the most common type of discrimination found in the UK. Racism and sexism are seen as unacceptable, but ageism is not seen as being as bad as these.

Evidence of differences in power and life-chances for different age groups

Young and old may experience ageism in the UK workplace.	Young people may be seen as not having experience, and are not given opportunities to gain it. Older people may be seen as forgetful or unable to deal with new technology.
There is an age crime curve which shows that younger people are more likely to be convicted of crime. They are also more likely to be victims when aged between 16 and 24.	The age crime curve shows that criminal activity begins in the teens and generally begins to decrease after the early 20s. This could be a result of stereotyping about youth by the agencies of social control. Moral panics may encourage the police to focus on youth. Older people may commit white-collar crime and be better at concealing their crimes.
The media is responsible for ageist stereotypes for both the young and the old.	The media has a long history of stereotyping and creating moral panics about youth. Stanley Cohen's *Folk Devils and Moral Panics* and Sarah Thornton's *Club Cultures* show classic examples of this.
	Older people are also scapegoated in newspapers. A *Daily Mail* headline in 2017 read that 'Bed-blocking "is causing 8000 deaths every year"', while the *Daily Express* in 2018 referred to 'Britain's ageing timebomb'.
Health is an area where there are differences in the experiences of young and old.	Being less physically healthy is seen as part of becoming old. However, the negative stereotypes associated with old age can affect physical health. The Royal Society for Public Health report from 2018 highlighted how the media showed problems such as dementia in a negative way, having a harmful effect on older people's well-being.

Strengths of the argument that ageism affects the life-chances and power of young people are:

The life chances of young people are worse than the older generation as it has become very difficult for young people to become home owners.

Under 18s were not allowed to vote in the EU referendum or general elections.

Young people are more likely to be unemployed. This is likely to make them feel socially excluded.

The minimum wage is lower for under 25- and under 21-year-olds and does not exist at all for under 18s.

Young Minds charity criticised the government for spending only 1 per cent of the NHS budget on children's mental health. Only one in three young people will get the mental health help they need.

Weaknesses of the argument that ageism affects the life-chances and power of young people are:

Under 18s do not understand enough about politics to vote. It is sensible to wait until they are old enough to understand.

Functionalists would argue that young people need to play a part in society by working for lower wages.

Older people have more responsibilities and need a secure wage.

The government has passed the Equality Act 2010 which protects young people from ageism.

Strengths of the argument that ageism affects the life-chances and power of older people are:

In the UK, older people lose status in society as they get beyond retirement age.

Stereotypes and negative views are constant in the media. A University of Southern California study found that half of elderly characters were referred to negatively using words such as 'frail', 'relic' or 'senile'.

In 2018, The Centre for Ageing Better criticised the UK as discriminating against older workers and providing poor training opportunities.

Weaknesses of the argument that ageism affects the life-chances and power of older people are:

Laws about age discrimination are now a key part of UK law.

Older people are often found in positions of power. Between 1979 and 2017 the average age of MPs was around 50.

Social attitudes are changing. Charities like Age UK provide advice for how to make the most of retirement. Life expectancy has increased, and old age starts later and lasts for longer.

employment
AGEISM
Sample text text could go here
Sample text text could go here
Sample text text could go here

OVER 50

Ageism discriminates against youth and older people and may leave people with a short window to get the best jobs.

Spec spotlight

5.3 Equality/inequality in relation to ethnicity

5.4 Factors which may influence access to life-chances and power: prejudice, discrimination, stereotyping, labelling, scapegoating, media representation, moral panics; with specific reference to ethnicity; racism, institutional racism

Link to textbook

pp 160–161: Issues of race and ethnicity in 21st-century UK

pp 162–163: How does the media portray different ethnic groups?

pp 164–165: How does ethnicity affect life-chances?

AO2 Apply

The figures refer to the per cent of students receiving exclusions from school in 2017.

	per cent of students with a fixed term exclusion	per cent of students permanently excluded
Bangladeshi	2.05	0.04
Indian	0.9	0.02
Pakistani	2.75	0.07
Black Caribbean	10.08	0.29
Black African	4.42	0.09
White	5.14	0.10
Mixed ethnicity	5.98	0.14
Chinese	0.56	0.01

Source https://www.ethnicity-facts-figures.service.gov.uk/education-skills-and-training/absence-and-exclusions/pupil-exclusions/latest

Which groups are most likely to be excluded from school?

How would you explain the figures for some of the groups?

Take it further

What else would you want to know that the figures do not tell you?

Ethnicity and inequality

Race and ethnicity are not the same.	The idea of different races is linked to biology. The idea of race has often been misused to justify racism, e.g. Hitler and the Jews. Ethnicity is used by sociologists and refers to people's culture and may include nationality, religion, traditions and way of life.
The UK is a society which contains very diverse ethnic groups. This is a result of the UK's history of being invaded but also having had a global empire.	The UK has struggled at times to live up to the welcome that it offered the individuals who lived in other parts of the British Empire after the Second World War. Racism has been a concern on two levels. There are minority far-right groups who attempt to cause conflict through racist propaganda. However, in some ways a greater concern has been the persistence of institutional racism shown in the Stephen Lawrence case and identified in the Macpherson Report.
Racism includes prejudice and discrimination against people because of their race, ethnicity, nationality and/or religion. Legislation has been passed which has aimed to reduce racism and discrimination in the UK.	Many laws have been passed promoting equality for people regardless of their ethnic background. The 1965 Race Relations Act banned racial discrimination in public places and the promotion of hatred related to colour, race, ethnicity or nationality. The act failed to protect ethnic minorities from discrimination when trying to secure jobs or housing. There were further race relations acts in 1968, 1976 and 2000. In 1976 the CR (Commission for Racial Equality) was set up. Sociologists would question how successful they have been.
The impact of the referendum on Brexit has pushed issues about immigration and racism into the news. The coalition government in 2010 set itself targets to reduce immigration by a set amount.	Membership of the European Union included free movement of EU citizens to live and work anywhere in the EU. Supporters of this, including many businesses, argued that this helped the UK's economy and allowed us to fill key jobs in areas like the NHS. The coalition government was pressured to reduce numbers coming to the UK. This has not been easy to achieve and has created unease for ethnic minorities.

Evidence of differences in power and life-chances for different ethnic groups

The pressure to lower immigration figures by David Cameron and Theresa May's governments resulted in a 'hostile environment' policy.	The 'hostile environment' policy resulted in the Home Office pressuring people to prove their right to live in the UK. This has resulted in tragic consequences for members of some ethnic groups including EU citizens and former immigrants. The Windrush scandal showed that immigrants who came to Britain in the 1950s and 60s were asked to produce documentation for employers, hospitals and landlords. Some were wrongly forced to leave the country. Other ethnic groups may worry about the effect on their lives in future.
There is a long-standing ethnic pay gap between different groups, according to the Equality and Human Rights Commission, 2017.	A 2018 pay audit in London found pay gaps of up to 37 per cent for some ethnic groups. London fire brigade was the only organisation with a 0 per cent ethnic pay gap. The main cause of the pay gap was the lack of ethnic minorities in higher-paid jobs, possibly due to institutional racism.
The media still under-represents or stereotypes ethnic minorities, women and disabled people in the news.	Ofcom carried out a 2017 study. The study found that ethnic minorities, disabled people and women were less likely to have jobs in television media and even less likely to have a top job. People from these groups would not feel connected to the media
People from ethnic minority groups still face discrimination by the law.	A government report in 2018 found that black, Asian and mixed race people were one and a half more times likely to be arrested than white people and more likely to be victims of crime. The Runnymede Trust argued that discrimination is part of police practice.

Strengths of the argument that ethnic minority groups' life-chances are improving are:

Six per cent of MPs elected in 2015 were non-white. This is ten times as many as in 1987.

In spring 2018, MI6, the secret intelligence service, used a young black mother in its advertisement for recruits. People associate MI6 with the white male 'James Bond' type. They are reaching out for ethnic minority and female applicants.

The government website gov.uk showed that the 'employment rate gap' between ethnic minorities and everyone else has closed from 15 per cent in 2004 to 10 per cent in 2016.

Weaknesses of the argument that ethnic minority groups' life-chances are improving are:

Ethnic minorities have higher unemployment rates than other groups.

A government report in 2017 showed that black people are three times more likely to be arrested than other ethnic groups.

Two out of three Indian and white people own their own homes. Fewer than half of African-Caribbean, Bangladeshi or other mixed backgrounds own their own homes according to a 2017 government report.

Explain reasons why individuals may be racist.

Strengths of the argument that prejudice and discrimination towards ethnic minority groups is less common are:

Laws about discrimination are now a key part of UK law and well known.

Diversity in the media is improving. Marvel comics have introduced a black Spiderman and Captain America. Action figures offer positive role models for children.

The Macpherson Report following the Stephen Lawrence case has made hospitals, schools and other institutions look at their practice.

Weaknesses of the argument that prejudice and discrimination towards ethnic minority groups is still common are:

Ethnic minority groups are still scapegoated in the media. Moral panics are created about gangs, knife crime and terrorism.

Racism is not always a conscious decision. People may not be aware of it.

A survey by *The Independent* newspaper in April 2018 found that less than half of ethnic minority people believed that progress on reducing prejudice had been made in the 25 years since Stephen Lawrence's death.

There is great variety in population ethnicity within the UK. Places like Birmingham, London, Manchester and large towns may be very diverse compared to smaller towns and villages.

Think link

The links with education and crime are obvious here. How does family link? Can the family of ethnic minorities affect life-chances?

Key figure

Tony Sewell, a British sociologist, has spent his career examining reasons for the under-achievement of African-Caribbean boys compared to their potential.

- Sewell blames the failure of African-Caribbean boys on the peer group they belong to.
- The peer group they belong to values the 'street' more than education.
- Sewell says that racism of teachers and/or institutional racism is not the problem.
- Sewell set up a successful Generating Genius programme which encouraged high-ability African-Caribbean boys to do science and engineering. This created a 'science gang' which gave them a new peer group with high expectations, where they aimed to be the best scientist.

Knowledge check

1. Outline what is meant by 'ethnicity'. **(2 marks)**
2. Identify two ways that stereotyping can affect life-chances. **(4 marks)**
3. Give reasons why some ethnic minority groups may be less equal in terms of wealth. **(4 marks)**
4. 'Ethnicity does not affect life-chances.' Do you agree? **(9 marks)**

Spec spotlight

5.3 Equality/inequality in relation to disability and sexuality

5.4 Factors which may influence access to life-chances and power: social construction of identity/roles/status, prejudice, discrimination, stereotyping, labelling, media representation, moral panics; with specific reference to disability, medical and social models of disability; with specific reference to sexuality, homophobia

Link to textbook

pp 166–167: How is disability viewed in our society?

pp 168–169: How does disability affect life-chances?

pp 170–171: Changing attitudes to sexuality in the UK

pp 172–173: How does sexuality affect life-chances?

AO2 Apply

A sociologist wanted to study attitudes towards disability through structured interviews. The researcher is a wheelchair user. How might this affect the research?

♿ Not all ♿ disabilities are visible

Disability includes a wide range of physical and mental impairments which may prevent people doing everyday tasks.

Take it further

Design the questions that could be included. What would be the advantages and disadvantages of this method?

Disability and life-chances

Sociologists have more recently begun to study other forms of social difference, including disability.	It is important to use language that is accepted by the people that are being referred to. 'Disabled people' is the accepted term to use. This term refers to people who are unable to do everyday tasks as well as others because of a physical or mental impairment. Therefore, it includes wheelchair users, people with learning difficulties, hearing and visual impairment, autism and other impairments.
Prejudice and discrimination about disability are an ongoing problem in the UK and other countries. This impacts upon life-chances.	People in society may find disability uncomfortable to talk about. Scope, the disabled charity, found that two-thirds of people found it difficult to talk to disabled people. A quarter of disabled people experienced prejudice as people expected less of them because of their disability.
There are two models of disability: the medical and social model. Disabled people have championed the social model to try and change the way that they are treated.	The medical model sees disability as a problem which needs to be cured. It is almost as if the disabled person is the problem as they do not match the norms of society. This can result in social exclusion for disabled people.
	The social model sees the focus on society as helping disabled people to overcome their impairment. Providing hearing loops, ramps, lifts and other support would be part of this model. The social model is about the rights of disabled people to take a full part in social life and be socially included.
There have been concerns about media reporting which labelled disabled people as lazy and taking advantage of the benefit system.	Phillip Hammond, the MP and Chancellor of the Exchequer, made remarks in December 2017 about low productivity in the economy, being partly due to more disabled people in the workforce. His comments caused a storm of protest from disabled charities, such as Scope. Comments like this are likely to increase prejudice and discrimination of disabled people in the workplace.

Sexuality and life-chances

Sexuality refers to a person's sexual orientation. Homophobia is prejudice and/or discrimination towards someone because of their homosexual orientation.	Social norms towards sexual orientation and transgender issues have changed very quickly since the end of the 20th century. However, prejudice and discrimination may still be common and as difficult to prove as ever.
Life-chances in the UK have traditionally been affected by a person not being heterosexual.	Laws discriminated against people from the gay community and denied them human rights. Homosexual acts were illegal in the UK until the Sexual Offences Act 1967. It took until 2001 before new laws reduced the age of consent from 21 to 16, giving gay people the same rights as heterosexual people.
	Same-sex marriage was made legal in 2014 making life-chances more equal.
LGBT is the term used to cover people from the lesbian, gay, bisexual and transgender communities.	Many new laws have now been passed which attempt to protect the rights of people in these groups. Transgender is recognised in the Equality Act 2010.
The media have presented LGBT people in a stereotypical way in general. Stereotypes of LGBT people are very complex, but some of these are that gay men act in a feminine way and are promiscuous. Lesbians are presented as 'butch' or manly.	The powerful story of *Moonlight* won an Oscar for best picture in 2017. A story with a black gay main character was rare and seen as ground-breaking. GLAAD (Gay and Lesbian Alliance against Defamation) reported that television shows streaming in November 2017 had the highest ever number of LGBT characters.

Strengths of the argument that there is less prejudice and discrimination towards disability are:

The Equality Act 2010 has made clear that disability is a protected characteristic. Discrimination is illegal.

Due to the Equality Act 2010, employers need to make reasonable adjustments to allow disabled people to do their jobs successfully.

Employers who do not do this are liable to be taken to court.

Disabled characters are much more common in soaps and films. This is making disabled people feel more included in society. Hopefully, this will make non-disabled people more informed and less uncomfortable talking to disabled people.

Weaknesses of the argument that there is less prejudice and discrimination towards disability are:

A BBC report in June 2018 showed a 50 per cent rise in the level of disability-related hate crime 2017/18.

There is a disability pay gap reported by the Trade Union Council in 2015.

Marxists say that disabled people are not seen as of value to capitalism. The extra cost of making reasonable adjustments of ramps or other changes will not be supported by employers who are interested in profit.

Strengths of the argument that there is less prejudice and discrimination towards different sexualities are:

The Equality Act 2010 has made clear that sexual orientation and transsexual are protected characteristics. Discrimination is illegal.

The UK had homophobic laws against homosexuality until 1967 and laws still did not treat gay and lesbian people equally. Now there is more equality.

In 1987 the government introduced Clause 28 which meant that schools could not be seen to be promoting sexuality. Clause 28 was repealed in 2003 by the Labour government.

Nowadays Ofsted checks whether schools are promoting mutual respect and tolerance through British values.

Weaknesses of the argument that there is less prejudice and discrimination towards different sexualities are:

Anti-LGBT bullying remains common in schools and LGBT people face higher rates of mental health issues compared to heterosexuals.

In September 2016, *MailOnline* branded same-sex pedestrian lights in Trafalgar Square in London as 'dangerous'.

The Independent in 2016 argued that the British media still features negative stories about LGBT people. The *Daily Express* tweeted that openly gay Olympic diver Tom Daley was to 'marry' in inverted commas, suggesting it was not a real marriage.

Strengths of the argument that social differences, such as disability and sexuality, affect life-chances and inequality are:

Homophobic bullying in schools has long-term effects on life-chances.

Many schools are not equipped to take disabled students, reducing their life-chances.

Hate crime has become a concern in the UK. LGBT and disabled people have been affected by this. *The Independent* reported in 2017 that one in five LGBT people reported verbal or physical attacks in the previous year.

George Gerbner found that the media either negatively stereotype gays, do not show them realistically or ignore them.

Weaknesses of the argument that social differences, such as disability and sexuality, affect life-chances and inequality are:

Awareness has become greater and is backed up by law.

The media is much more diverse and shows disabled and LGBT characters.

Young people are much more open to diversity than the older generation, meaning things may continue to improve. Schools and other agencies of socialisation are promoting British values of tolerance and mutual respect.

Key figure

Barnes (1992) argued in *Disabling Imagery and the Media: An Exploration of Media Representations of Disabled People*, that the media shows disabled people in a negative way. The media shows disabled people in several common ways:
- in need of help
- as victims
- as villains, criminals or monsters
- as a burden
- as 'super cripples' overcoming difficulties
- but never as normal people who just happen to have a disability.

INTERNATIONAL DAY AGAINST HOMOPHOBIA AND TRANSPHOBIA

Protest on these issues is a huge global movement. Laws about issues such as gay marriage still vary around the world.

Think link

How does this topic link to the topic of deviance?

Knowledge check

1. Outline what is meant by 'homophobia'. **(2 marks)**
2. Define what is meant by 'moral panic'. **(4 marks)**
3. Give reasons why sexual orientation may affect life-chances. **(4 marks)**
4. 'Disability is one of the main causes of inequality in the UK today.' Do you agree? **(9 marks)**

AO2 Apply

The government has set aside money to address the issue of child poverty. Which of these are about addressing material deprivation and which cultural deprivation? Are any of them both?

- Reading books
- Free entry to museums and castles for poorer families
- Learning mentors in schools
- Careers education from Year 7
- Free breakfasts and dinners for poorer children
- Selective schools for the cleverest poorer children
- French lessons for Years 1 and 2
- Nursery funding
- Homework clubs
- Free iPads

Can you rank them from 1 to 10?
1 = Highest priority down to
10 = lowest priority.

Take it further

Explain your choice in a paragraph. Refer to sociological theories.

How is poverty defined?

Poverty

Poverty has been a UK concern since Victorian times.	Poverty is a global issue. Interestingly, a lot of the research began in the UK, one of the richest countries in the world, especially at the time of the research by Booth, Rowntree and others.
Poverty can be measured in different ways. There are two main ideas about what poverty is: absolute and relative poverty.	Poverty is socially constructed: our idea about what it is changes from place to place and time to time. Absolute poverty: a person has no access to their basic needs of food, water, shelter, clothing and warmth. Relative poverty: a person's living conditions are not as good as expected in that society. In 21st-century UK, our expectations include having wi-fi!
Expectations of how individuals and families live have changed over time. Sociologists have studied both material and cultural deprivation.	Material deprivation: not having the things needed to live a good life. Can be fixed by buying the goods that people don't have. Cultural deprivation: lacking the values, knowledge and ideas needed to succeed. Some children grow up in families who do not have the right knowledge and values to help their children break out of poverty. For example, children who are not taught the value of reading by their parents could be seen as lacking something of great importance in their life.
Growing up in poverty has been shown to have long-term effects on the life-chances of children.	Children who grow up in poverty may become trapped in a cycle of deprivation. They are likely to lack the education needed to break out of poverty and may not learn the value of education. Their children grow up the same and so the cycle continues.

Sociological views of poverty

Functionalists view all parts of social life, including poverty, as having a positive role for society.	Herbert Gans argues that society needs the very low-paid workers to help companies make a profit. They also need people to do unpopular, unpleasant or dangerous jobs. The threat of poverty motivates people to do these jobs. Sometimes poverty may only be a temporary problem and will make the government realise that they need to do something to create more jobs or help the poor.
The New Right see poverty as the fault of the poor themselves who are not prepared to work hard, and also the government for paying benefits too readily.	Charles Murray is an American New Right sociologist who strongly supports the view that the poor have a culture (way of life) which means they are choosing to stay in poverty. David Marsland (1989), a British sociologist, says that charities like the Joseph Rowntree Foundation exaggerate poverty. Benefits encourage people not to work. Marsland is critical of the whole of sociology for exaggerating inequality.
Marxists blame capitalism for poverty. It is a greedy system which results in extreme poverty. The ruling class benefit from the very poor working for low wages.	Poverty means that there is a group of workers who are desperate and prepared to work for low wages. Marxists therefore see poverty as helping capitalism. It is also an inevitable part of a social system that is based on greed.
Globalisation has an effect on poverty in the UK. It can help to reduce poverty, but some people are concerned about the effects of globalisation.	Global trade has brought the world closer together and companies from all over the world may choose to base themselves in the UK. Children in the UK now have a much wider variety of foods available to give them a better diet. International trade can flourish. On the other hand, Marxists worry that globalisation has damaged job security as multinational companies can easily move to another country costing jobs. Marxists also say that multinationals want to pay low wages and give workers few rights. The low paid may risk unemployment and poverty.

Strengths of the functionalist view of poverty are:		
It explains why poverty exists.	It suggests that it is possible to work your way out of poverty through education and hard work.	Accepts that the government sometimes needs to do something to help people in poverty, e.g. boosting the economy and creating more jobs.

Weaknesses of the functionalist view of poverty are:		
Functionalists are biased and see poverty as a good thing.	It is difficult to see how society can get rid of poverty if it plays a positive role.	It ignores the harm that poverty does to the life-chances of many children. This damages society and wastes talent.

Strengths of the Marxist view of poverty are:		
It challenges the growing inequality in the UK.	It promises an end to poverty.	Offers explanation for the whole of society's problems.

Weaknesses of the Marxist view of poverty are:		
Marxists do not consider that poverty may not be possible to stop as there will always be people who do not work hard enough.	It has an overly negative view of society.	They do not offer a real solution for the problems. Marxist societies have not worked well.

Strengths of Peter Townsend's work on poverty are:		
Townsend is very influential on the study of poverty.	It made a deprivation index which gave a practical method of studying poverty.	It showed how relative poverty affected people's ability to take part in society.

Weaknesses of Peter Townsend's work on poverty are:		
His work is outdated as it is from the 1970s.	His deprivation index is based on his view. One thing on it was eating a cooked breakfast. Not eating a cooked breakfast is a matter of choice, not a sign of poverty.	Relative deprivation or poverty is all very well, but all Townsend does is show inequality. Functionalists say that we have to have inequality.

Food banks have become more common in the years since the 2008 banking crisis. The Independent reported use of food banks at the highest ever in 2018.

Key figure

Oscar Lewis studied families living in poverty in Mexico. He published his book *Five Families: Mexican Case Studies in the Culture of Poverty* in 1959. His study introduced the idea of a culture of poverty. He found that the families felt helpless, powerless and dependent living on the edges of society. They became used to this way of life which offered them no route out.

Think link

Check that you know Pat Carlen's study on women, poverty and crime.

Knowledge check

1. Identify two types of material deprivation. **(2 marks)**
2. Define what is meant by 'poverty'. **(4 marks)**
3. Give reasons why poverty is hard to escape. **(4 marks)**
4. 'Poverty is one of the great social issues in the UK today.' Do you agree? **(9 marks)**

Spec spotlight

AO2 Apply

Examples of social inclusion policies which the government have used include:

- *trying to close the gap between the disadvantaged and the better off at school*
- *school leaving age raised to 18*
- *more careers education*
- *free public transport*
- *nursery education for all*
- *encourage employers to give jobs to socially excluded groups*
- *reduce the number of jobs with low pay.*

Explain how these policies would include different groups based on class, gender, ethnicity, disability, age or other groups.

Take it further

Consider whether you would increase benefits or reduce them. Which would have the greatest effect on social exclusion?

What would the theories say?

Social inclusion and exclusion

Social exclusion is the idea that some groups and individuals are not able to fully take part in social life.	In the 1970s, a person without a television would have felt excluded from a large part of social life. Being without a job, transport or not able to take a holiday could also make it difficult for a group to feel part of society.
Social inclusion is about the efforts made to ensure that people are not excluded and fully able to participate in social life.	Social inclusion is seen as a priority by the UK government. Promoting it successfully could change elements of UK society, e.g. loneliness and isolation of older people, gang membership of young people, unemployment, health, crime and poverty. A government press release in late 2017, the government admitted that 20 years of such policies had not been successful. The best successes were in promoting employment and encouraging working-class children to go to university, but there were groups who felt left out.
A number of groups in the UK are vulnerable to social exclusion and poverty. These include the working class, women, disabled, ethnic minorities and older people.	Feminists argue that women are most likely to end up in poverty, due to several reasons. They are often responsible for childcare, limiting the amount and type of work they can do. The gender pay gap also affects women, meaning their wages are more likely to be low. Prejudice and discrimination mean other groups also have a pay gap. Society has made efforts to socially include such groups. This includes making reasonable adjustments for disabled people at work.
Sociologists have noted the growth of a group called the underclass.	The underclass is seen as beneath the class system. May be homeless, long-term unemployed or criminal. The mass unemployment in the 1980s was the background to this first being seen in the UK and social exclusion became a growing concern.

The culture of poverty

The culture of poverty is the idea that people living in poverty develop a way of living that helps them survive.	The culture of poverty was first identified by Oscar Lewis, who studied families in Mexico. It includes managing on little money and building a lifestyle based on this. Crime may be a way of managing to survive. Cheap alcohol and drugs may provide sufficient entertainment to pass the time. Charles Murray visited the UK in 1989 and claimed that an underclass, with a culture of poverty, was growing here.
The culture of poverty has a set of values that do not help people escape from poverty.	Charles Murray is a New Right thinker: values of the underclass is the culture of poverty. Focus on short-term success (immediate gratification with no long-term goals or a plan for improving their lives. As parents, the underclass were not successful in school and do not encourage their children to be so.
The New Right are very critical of society for encouraging people living in poverty to be dependent through welfare benefits.	Society has encouraged this group to be dependent by paying benefits to people who are sick or out of work. The New Right argue that if people do not work then the state will pay them benefits and they do not have to work.
The New Right also blame the poor themselves for choosing to live in the culture of poverty.	Charles Murray is also very critical of the culture of poverty. He blames the underclass for having a lifestyle that takes advantage of benefits and uses crime to live a lifestyle that is lazy and immoral. The underclass underachieve in school, take poor care of their own health and that of their children, turn to drugs and crime and pass on these values to their children. His view is that they contribute nothing to society and take advantage of benefits and a free national health service.

Strengths of the New Right view of the underclass are:

There has been a group of long-term unemployed in the UK since the 1980s.

Efforts to improve the life-chances of the underclass through education have not been as successful as hoped. This shows how deep the culture of poverty may be.

Benefits are costing the UK a great deal of money.

Weaknesses of the New Right view of the underclass are:

This is an unfair view of many poorer people in the UK who work hard for low pay and in insecure jobs.

Murray looks down on the culture of the poor.

Marxists would say that the existence of the poor is a result of capitalism. The rich are making huge profits while the poor suffer. Crime is a result of an unequal society.

Taking benefits away would result in children suffering from extreme hardship and absolute poverty. As one of the wealthiest countries in the world it is not acceptable.

Social inclusion means that everyone is able to participate in social life.

Strengths of the Marxist view of the underclass are:

Marx predicted that inequality would get worse. The underclass is a sign of this.

Marxism explains rising crime levels as the underclass turn to crime as a form of rebellion against capitalism. This may explain rising crime levels.

It puts forward a social justice view that the rich do not deserve to have everything while the poor have nothing.

Weaknesses of the Marxist view of the underclass are:

It does not consider the fact that some people may not want to work and are happy to take benefits.

There has not been a revolution even with the great inequality shown by the underclass.

It ignores gender and ethnicity. Racism adds to the problems of ethnic groups who are part of the underclass.

Which groups are most likely to be unemployed?

Key figures

J. Rex and S. Tomlinson (1979), in a study of Handsworth in Birmingham, discovered that ethnic minority groups were part of an underclass beneath the white working class. They were disadvantaged in jobs, housing and education. The groups also experienced hostility and racism which added to the difficulties they faced.

Think link

How does gender affect social exclusion? Does the greater social control of women (Frances Heidensohn) make women more likely to be socially excluded? What about the fact that women are more likely to be responsible for young children? Live in poverty? Have lower-paid work?

Knowledge check

1. Outline what is meant by 'underclass'. **(2 marks)**

2. Define what is meant by 'culture of poverty'. **(4 marks)**

3. Explain why some groups may be socially excluded. **(4 marks)**

4. Discuss how society could promote social inclusion. **(9 marks)**

Spec spotlight

5.1 Sociological theories of stratification: Functionalist theory of stratification, Davis and Moore's theory on the role of stratification in terms of effective role allocation linked to the promise of rewards, meritocracy, Marxist theory of social stratification, feminist views on patriarchy and stratification

Link to textbook

pp 126–127: Functionalist views on stratification
Ideas from the whole of Chapter 4 and Chapter 3 Education

AO2 Apply

Can you think of barriers that prevent meritocracy from being fair? What stops some talented people from being successful?

Take it further

Does it matter whether the UK is a meritocracy or not? What happens if working-class talent does not achieve success? What other groups may be disadvantaged? What will happen to the UK as we try to compete with the rest of the world?

Meritocracy

Meritocracy is the idea that effort + ability = reward.	A meritocracy is a society where people who have talent and ability and who work hard should gain the highest rewards.
If a society is a meritocracy then rewards are given fairly to those who deserve them. Inequality is necessary to have a meritocracy.	Functionalists believe that society will work best as a meritocracy. The brightest and best people will work hard and produce the best outcomes for society. The cleverest people will want to be scientists, doctors and leaders working to improve society because of the high rewards.
The unequal rewards given to the best are needed by society in the functionalist view.	If a meritocracy is working properly then a person's gender, social class or ethnic group should not matter. Society needs the best people to succeed.
The high amounts of wages and rewards for top jobs mean that roles are allocated to the best people.	K. Davis and W.E. Moore called this effective role allocation. In their view people who work hard at school to get qualifications will get the best rewards as adults.

Meritocracy in a changing UK

For meritocracy to work there have to be opportunities for people to move up the class system, e.g. working-class people can become middle class or even upper class.	A society where it is possible to climb the class system is known as an open society. The ability to move up the class system is known as social mobility.
In the UK there was a great deal of social mobility in the 1950s and 1960s.	After the Second World War ended there were a lot more jobs available in areas like health, education and the civil service. These jobs were non-manual and required educated people. This helped many working-class people to become middle class. There was very little unemployment at this time.
Education was freely available to all and more people began to go to university including working-class people.	Unfortunately, since the late 1970s unemployment has been a much greater problem. There have not been as many jobs available. This has meant that it is harder to break into the top jobs. The larger numbers going to university may also make it more competitive.
In the 21st century all governments in the UK have been concerned about the poor life-chances of what they describe as the 'disadvantaged'.	There may be many more people who could be classed as middle class, but it may be harder than ever to break out of the working class. Young people have to pay tuition fees for university now and take a loan. This may discourage some young people from trying for the very best jobs.

Gender inequality is one thing stopping the UK being a meritocracy. What others can you think of?

Strengths of the argument that the UK is a meritocracy are:

The UK is one of the top world economies. Talent is obviously being motivated by the rewards on offer.

Numbers going to university are much bigger than in the 1960s. This includes more working-class people. People like Alan Sugar show that anything is possible.

Women are becoming more successful. This shows that talent is becoming more likely to be rewarded whether you are male or female.

Weaknesses of the argument that the UK is a meritocracy are:

Feminists argue that the glass ceiling still exists, preventing women reaching the top jobs. Many women with talent do not achieve what they deserve.

Institutional racism is still well documented in many parts of British life. Although over twenty years since the Macpherson Report, it may still be difficult for some ethnic minority groups to avoid discrimination when applying for jobs.

Pay gaps exist for ethnicity, gender and disability. One of the main causes of this is said to be not being able to access the better-paid jobs and higher positions. In a meritocracy this would not happen.

Strengths of the Marxist view that the UK is not a meritocracy are:

The old boys' network shows that there is no meritocracy. People who go to private school are more likely to be MPs and achieve other high positions in society.

Cultural capital gives the middle classes an advantage. The children from better backgrounds have an advantage from the help their parents are able to give them.

Marxists argue that schools prepare the working class for their jobs as cheap labour to keep the ruling class wealthy.

Weaknesses of the Marxist view that the UK is not a meritocracy are:

School exams are a fair system of judging the best students. Anyone can be successful, regardless of class, gender or ethnicity, if they have the ability and make the effort.

Anyone can borrow the money to go to university. The debt is cancelled if the student never makes over £21,000. Therefore, anyone has an opportunity.

The government has spent lots of money on closing the gap between disadvantaged students and everybody else. It spends over £900 per pupil per year. This represents thousands of pounds in the schools with the poorest children. Ofsted is harsh on schools if they do not use this money well.

Key figure

Michael Young wrote a book in 1958 called *The Rise of the Meritocracy*. He imagined a society where intelligence and achievement were highly valued and rewarded. The problem was that the people at the bottom knew they were the least talented and felt themselves to be worthless. On the other hand those at the top were arrogant as they knew they were the best and deserved to be.

Think link

There are strong links between this topic and education. Make sure you know these links.

Knowledge check

1. Outline what is meant by 'social class'. (2 marks)
2. Define what is meant by 'meritocracy'. (4 marks)
3. Discuss the functionalist view of stratification. (9 marks)

Spec spotlight

6.1 Social construction of concepts of crime and deviance: what is crime? what is deviance? historical and cultural variations, social construction of crime and deviance

Link to textbook

pp 10–11:   Key sociological concepts (1)
pp 188–189: What are crime and deviance?
pp 190–191: Socially constructed concepts of crime and deviance

Individuals who act outside of social norms may be labelled as deviant. What do you think of this?

AO2 Apply

Find 5–10 examples of things which we would consider criminal or deviant that other societies would see as acceptable.

Take it further

Ask people who do not study sociology if there are any acts which are universally wrong. Try to persuade them that there is no such thing and crime and deviance are socially constructed.

What is deviance?

Deviance means the act of breaking a social norm.	Children learn quickly what social norms are. They recognise that breaking them may result in a sanction, e.g. babies are allowed to break social norms about eating and may end up with a bowl of baked beans all over their face. However, as they grow they are taught to follow the norms of eating.
Social norms are very complex, but people are able to recognise when they break them through the reactions of others.	The reactions of others to acts of deviance are known as sanctions. These range from informal sanctions, such as dirty looks, comments, turning their back on someone, to more formal sanctions, such as exclusion from school, fines and prison sentences.
What is seen as deviant varies over time and in different places.	The reason for this is because deviance is socially constructed. Deviance is created by society. For this reason, it is different in different cultures and at different times in history. For instance, forks only began to be used in Europe after the Italian Renaissance in the 16th century. There were expectations about manners even in medieval times, but they were slightly different. One 14th century writer advised not to clean your hands on the table cloth after spitting or blowing your nose.
Deviance and crime are not the same.	Some deviant acts may also be a crime. Some are not, and this can depend on the situation. Killing someone is normally seen as deviant and is a crime. When at war, killing may be seen as a good thing to do. It is still possible for it to be illegal in the case of a war crime.

What is crime?

Crime is an act which breaks the laws passed by the government.	Criminal acts are punishable through the courts. For instance, breaking into a house and stealing property is a crime and could result in prison. The sanctions used are likely to be formal.
What is classed as criminal varies over time and in different places.	Laws about smoking, driving and homosexuality have seen great changes over the past fifty years. Society changes and laws change to reflect this. The changes in technology have made many new crimes possible and laws are passed to stop them. The Malicious Communications Act 1988 covers comments which cause 'distress or anxiety' using technology. The Communications Act 2003 also offered further protection from what we now call internet 'trolls'.
People committing deviant acts can sometimes lead to changes in the law.	In the summer of 2018 the government made changes to the laws on the use of cannabis oil for medicinal purposes. This was following the activity of several families who were using it to improve the treatment of their children who were suffering from epilepsy. This was a big change for the government, but it stressed that there will be no relaxation of laws relating to any other use of cannabis. Martin Luther King advised his followers to protest by breaking laws to put pressure on the US government to stop discrimination against black people.
Who decides what is criminal or deviant?	Functionalists would say that what is seen as criminal or deviant is good for society and prevents acts which harm society. Marxists and feminists would argue that some groups (ruling class and men) are able to control what is seen as criminal or deviant.

Strengths of the functionalist view of crime and deviance are:

It explains how society works and why some acts are seen as criminal or deviant.

Having clear ideas about what is criminal or deviant makes society stronger. Functionalists call this value consensus and say it shows how people share an idea about right and wrong.

They explain how deviance can help society by leading to changes in social norms and the law. People who break social norms can be seen as paving the way for others. For example, gay people who broke the law when homosexual acts were illegal took enormous risks, but eventually the law and social norms changed.

Weaknesses of the functionalist view of crime and deviance are:

It ignores the power that some groups have to shape the law, e.g. men, ruling class, heterosexuals and white people.

Ignores the fact that judges are mainly men and older people.

Strengths of the conflict view of crime and deviance are:

Marxists consider how working-class people have little say in shaping laws.

Feminists show how females are controlled through social norms. Sanctions are put in place for women who act in a deviant way. This benefits men.

Shows how other weaker groups (ethnic minorities, disabled, LGBT) people may be considered deviant because they are different.

Weaknesses of the conflict view of crime and deviance are:

Marxists ignore ethnicity and gender.

Feminists ignore social class and ethnicity.

Sometimes the ruling class do not benefit when things are shown to be deviant or criminal, e.g. MPs' expenses scandal, PPI scandal, Google and Amazon tax.

Sometimes men do not benefit when society labels male behaviour as unacceptable, e.g. Harvey Weinstein and the #MeToo campaign.

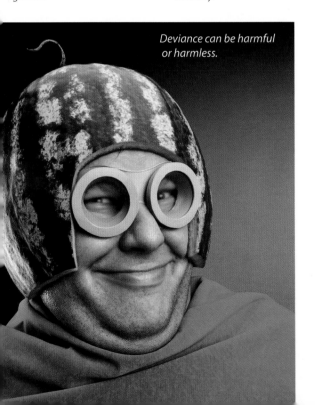

Deviance can be harmful or harmless.

Think link
This topic links closely to the first chapter and contains some of the most important ideas of sociology. Make sure you have revised topic one thoroughly before revising crime and deviance.

REVISION BOOSTER

One common mistake at Sociology GCSE has been to confuse the ideas of crime and deviance. Deviance is not necessarily criminal or 'bad'. A member of the public who risks their own life in a reckless way to save others may be seen as deviant, but also as a hero. A person suffering from mental illness may not break the law but may still be seen as different.

Check you know the difference by talking to other people about it, including your class and teacher.

Key figure

Howard Becker is an interactionist sociologist. He showed how a person could be labelled as deviant. A person committing an act of deviance (e.g. stealing) could be labelled as a deviant person. Becker explained that if they accepted this label and saw themselves as deviant they would begin a deviant career. In this case they would take on the label of thief and continue to act this out.

Knowledge check

1. Identify two acts that are criminal. **(2 marks)**
2. Outline what is meant by 'deviance'. **(4 marks)**
3. Give reasons for the variations in what different societies see as deviant. **(4 marks)**
4. Discuss which groups are able to decide what is seen as criminal. **(15 marks)**

Spec spotlight

5.2 Social control: informal and formal social control, agencies of social control, sanctions, role of the police and courts

Link to textbook

AO2 Apply

Sanctions may be positive as well as negative. Parents attempt to control their children with rewards.

Imagine a 20-year-old being sent to prison for robbery. Make a list of all the sanctions positive and negative that may have been applied by family, school and friends to try and persuade them away from a life of crime.

Take it further

Find out what happens when a person goes to prison. What sanctions are used to try to encourage them to reform and leave prison determined not to be a criminal?

Functionalists focus on the positive role that the police do. They deal with some of the most difficult problems and restore social order. For instance, when there is an accident on the roads.

What is informal social control?

Informal social control happens every day and we mostly do not think about it.	We exercise social control every day over other people, often without thinking. When someone acts in a way we do not want, we try to 'control' them by sanctions, e.g. someone who pushes into a queue will get dirty looks, 'tuts', comments or even raised voices. This is an attempt to get them to change their behaviour.
The family is one of the most important agencies of informal social control.	The family is the first place where social control takes place. Parents and other family members will impose sanctions when we act in ways they do not approve of. Family is still an important agency of social control when we are older. Schools will invite parents in when they are struggling to control a student.
There are several other agents of informal social control.	As we get older we experience other agencies of informal social control. School is often the first of these with both teachers and peers seeking to control our behaviour. Religion has been a very powerful source of informal social control. People who have been strongly socialised into a religion will find their conscience acting as a form of social control.
Informal agencies of social control are enough to control most individuals.	Informal agencies of social control are able to discourage people from breaking social norms by the use of sanctions. They may also discourage people from breaking the law as they fear social disapproval. Strong communities can create social control. Social media may also now play a role in this.

What is formal social control?

Formal social control happens when informal social control is not successful.	Agencies like the police, youth workers and schools work together to attempt to control young people who are getting out of society's control. This may involve informal warnings and could lead to formal sanctions including fines or prison. Having a criminal record is seen as a very negative thing and can place limits on other things a person can do. The media may also report on behaviour and publicly shame people.
Formal social control is organised in a systematic way with rules and procedures.	Laws are written down in a formal way and there are procedures to follow. Punishments have to be applied fairly and those accused are allowed a fair trial.
The police and courts are two of the most important agencies of social control.	The police and courts are part of the criminal justice system and are the main agencies for social control. Children's services may also enforce social control on families that endanger their children. However, they also do a lot of work with families to try to informally control them.
Consensus (functionalist) and conflict (Marxism and feminism) theories disagree about whether social control is a good thing or not.	Functionalists see social control as a positive thing which is necessary for society to function properly. Much of what is called informal social control would be seen as socialisation by functionalists. Marxists would see social control as a harsh means of making sure that the ruling class remain in control. The agencies of social control are controlled by the ruling class. The media ensures that the working class do not see that the police and courts are unfair. The working class suffer from false class consciousness and do not realise how unfair the system is. Feminists would see social control as being in favour of men. Social control maintains patriarchy and keeps men in a dominant position.

Strengths of the functionalist view of social control are:

It helps us to understand reasons when social control fails, e.g. riots, rise in crime rate.	It recognises the hard work done by police, courts and the legal system to keep society safe. Police also help to socialise children and the public in general.	Without social control, society would be in chaos. Agencies of social control help to keep order.

Weaknesses of the functionalist view of social control are:

The police were found to be institutionally racist in the Macpherson Report.	Ignores the ways in which police and courts may operate unfairly. Marxists criticise the police for unfairly targeting working-class people.	Judges do not represent the whole population in a balanced way. Feminists and others would see the courts as white, male, middle aged or elderly.

Strengths of the Marxist view of social control are:

They highlight the way that the courts and police favour the rich and powerful. The lack of judges from working-class backgrounds is a problem.	Marxists have raised important questions about corporate and white-collar crime which may harm the public. This has put pressure on the agencies of social control to target these as well, e.g. MPs' expenses scandal, PPI payments.	They raise important questions about the way that working-class people are treated by the police. The experiences of Hillsborough and Stephen Lawrence mean that we cannot assume the police will always be fair.

Weaknesses of the Marxist view of social control are:

Without the police, social order would collapse.	Marxism seems to forget that working-class people are also victims of working-class criminals. They might suffer more than most groups.	Communist countries which tried out Marxist ideas had even harsher forms of social control.

Strengths of the feminist view of social control are:

Exposes the way that women are still disadvantaged and limited by men.	Focuses on the different ways that girls and boys are socialised.	Radical feminists highlight the way that domestic violence and sexual offences control women as a whole.

Weaknesses of the feminist view of social control are:

Needs to consider that the experiences of ethnic minority women may be very different from those of white women.	Feminist ideas about social control are based on an out-of-date idea about how girls and women behave.	Martyn Denscombe found that male-type criminal behaviour by girls is more common than in the past.

Marxists see the police as enforcing social control in the interests of the rich and powerful.

Key figure

Emile Durkheim was a founder of sociology and a very important functionalist. He believed that social norms were very important to maintain social order. His idea of anomie means a situation where social norms to control behaviour do not exist, e.g. at times of war or riots. People are no longer controlled and will do things they would not normally do. Anomie means simply 'normlessness'.

Think link

The topic of social control appears in Chapter 1. It could also be related to the family. Social control over individual behaviour has relaxed in the last decades. For instance, cohabitation, abortion, divorce, remarriage and same-sex marriage used to result in sanctions. The Church of England has relaxed its views on some issues and may now allow divorced people to remarry in church, e.g. Prince Harry and Meghan Markle (who was divorced).

Knowledge check

1. What is the role of the police? **(2 marks)**
2. Outline what is meant by 'informal social control'. **(4 marks)**
3. Explain why religion can be an important part of social control. **(4 marks)**
4. Discuss whether social control is a positive part of society. **(15 marks)**

Spec spotlight

6.4 Sociological theories of deviance and criminal behaviour: consensus view of functionalism, anomie including the work of Merton and strain theory, subcultural theory, Albert Cohen and delinquent subcultures

AO2 Apply

What different subcultures are there in your local area? What are the norms and values of each subculture? Are they easy to understand from the outside? Are you part of a subculture, or more than one? What rewards do members of the subculture give each other?

Take it further

Ask your teacher/parent/carer/ older family member about what the subcultures were like when they young.

Or find out about Walter Miller's ideas about male subculture or a British version of this study by Howard Parker in Liverpool.

Functionalist and structural views of crime and deviance

Functionalists argue that crime plays a positive function (does something to help society work).	Crime and deviance show the rest of us the right way to behave. When someone commits a crime, it strengthens what Durkheim called the collective sentiments. The crowd that gathered to watch a hanging in the past and the crowd who gather to watch a notorious criminal arrive at court are being reminded about what the rest of us stand for. Even terrorist attacks like the ones in Paris and Manchester serve as a reminder to everyone else of what we believe in.
Functionalists argue that deviance plays a positive function (does something to help society work).	Deviance can point the way to how things will be done in future. This could be people having tattoos or piercings or challenging something that is wrong in society, e.g. Rosa Parks' bus boycott.
Robert K. Merton is a functionalist from the USA.	Robert K. Merton took Durkheim's idea of anomie and used it to explain crime in the USA. His ideas could be applied to the UK.
Robert K. Merton explained crime through the structures of society.	The structures Merton talked about were the goals of US society and the means of achieving them. He noticed that the idea of the American Dream was very important in the USA. However, there was an imbalance because people wanted the American Dream so badly, and there was not the means for everyone to succeed. Merton explained that people could respond in five different ways to this.

Subcultural views of crime and deviance

A subculture is a group within society with its own set of norms and values.	Subcultures are not always criminal. There are many non-criminal subcultures including train spotters, dog owners, cosplayers and many others. Sociologists have been particularly interested in youth subcultures which behave in a deviant way.
Albert Cohen developed a theory of why groups turned to crime using the idea of subcultures.	Cohen criticised Merton for not explaining crimes that do not make a profit, e.g. vandalism, joyriding, violence. Cohen tried to explain how groups turn to crime and develop their own set of norms and values.
Albert Cohen said that working-class people who feel anger at their position in society experience status frustration and join a deviant subculture.	The reason Cohen gave for the subculture was that working-class people suffer from material and cultural deprivation. This makes them unlikely to be successful in education or work. They experience status frustration which means they are frustrated at their position in society. They feel unsuccessful and unimportant.
Criminal subcultures have different norms to those of the rest of society.	Criminal subcultures turn the values of 'normal' society upside down. In a criminal subculture the values may include dishonesty, violence, lying and loyalty to the criminal group amongst others. This allows them to be successful in ways that society does not approve of, but it may take away their status frustration.

Popular BBC series Peaky Blinders *imagined a criminal gang based in Birmingham in the 1920s. What were the norms and values of the criminal subculture? What made the characters turn to crime? Are there other TV shows and films that show a criminal subculture? What were these like?*

Strengths of the functionalist view of crime and deviance are:

Explains how a small amount of crime is natural and inevitable. We can never have a crime-free society.	Helps us understand social changes. Helps us understand the role of punishment.	Makes sense when we think of the solidarity that takes place as a result of an attack like the one at Ariana Grande's concert in Manchester in 2017. The reaction was to show the terrorists our solidarity. The Queen strongly condemned the terrorists. The Manchester community helped the survivors and held another concert, 'One Love', a month later to show our solidarity. Celebrities took part to show their support.

Weaknesses of the functionalist view of crime and deviance are:

Surely crime cannot be a good thing. It is harmful to society. Too rosy a view of society and people.	Ignores the fact that some crime benefits the rich, e.g. corporate crime.	Durkheim did not explain why some groups turn to crime.

Strengths of strain theory are:

Merton has had a great influence on the sociology of crime, adapting Durkheim's ideas.	Merton's strain theory explains different types of crime.	Merton was being critical of the greed that drives society. Sometimes functionalists are accused of ignoring problems.

Weaknesses of strain theory are:

Assumes that everyone has the same values. Working-class people may not want the same type of success as middle-class people.	Marxists say strain theory blames crime on the working class. Corporate crime is ignored.	Merton saw crime as an individual response. Cohen saw it as a group response.

Strengths of Cohen's subcultural view are:

Explains why criminal subcultures form.	Useful for explaining youth crime and gang culture.	The theory is useful in understanding the reasons why people may turn to crime. Resources can be put into working with young people in particular to improve how they feel about themselves.

Weaknesses of Cohen's subcultural view are:

Does not explain lone criminals.	Ignores the fact that being poor may push people towards crime.	Only explains working-class crime. Ignores corporate crime and that committed by the higher social classes.

REVISION BOOSTER

The 9-mark questions in this chapter require evaluation and discussion. You need to bring in ideas from other sections of the chapter, especially for pages like this one on the causes of crime. Try writing a plan for them at the end of the page, but make sure that you come back to the plans and add more ideas.

Key figure

Robert K. Merton outlined five different ways that people could respond to their failure to achieve the goal of the American Dream. These were conformity, ritualism, innovation, retreatism and rebellion.

Conformity and ritualism represent giving up on success in slightly different ways. Innovation explains turning to crime to achieve the goals in criminal ways. Retreatism could involve deviant and criminal behaviour. A person gives up so turns to alcohol or drugs. Rebellion could explain terrorism as a response to failing to achieve the goals of US society.

Think link

Notice the links between Cohen's ideas and the topic of pro- and anti-school subcultures in education. His explanations of crime could be used in a school context as well. Those students who are not prefects, good at academic subjects or in the school team may feel frustrated at their low status and create their own anti-school subculture.

Knowledge check

1. Identify two features of criminal subcultures. **(2 marks)**
2. Outline what is meant by 'strain theory'. **(4 marks)**
3. Explain why functionalists believe that some crime is useful for society. **(4 marks)**
4. Discuss the importance of subcultures as an explanation for crime. **(15 marks)**

A riot is a situation in which norms and values may not apply. How might being part of a crowd add to this?

Spec spotlight

6.4 Sociological theories and explanations of deviance and criminal behaviour: conflict view of Marxism , Chambliss and differential enforcement of the law, white-collar and corporate crime

Link to textbook

pp 212–213: How does Marxism explain crime?

pp 214–215: What is white-collar crime?

pp 216–217: What is corporate crime?

Capitalism creates winners and losers. Those in poverty are more likely to turn to crime.

AO2 Apply

These are 10 different crimes. How would Marxists explain them?

- *Shoplifting*
- *Graffiti*
- *Assault*
- *Domestic violence*
- *Tax evasion by a big business*
- *Gang violence*
- *Trolling – harassment on the internet*
- *Voting illegally in an election e.g. more than one vote*
- *Joyriding*
- *Underage drinking*

Take it further

How would the other theories you know explain these?

What is the Marxist view of crime?

Marxists believe that crime is a result of capitalism.	Capitalism is the name for the economic system of the UK and many other countries, including the EU and the USA. It involves the pursuit of profit through buying and selling goods. People are encouraged to be successful by becoming rich.
Consumerism is a key part of capitalism and people are persuaded to buy goods which makes the bourgeoisie (ruling class) rich.	Consumerism convinces people that they want goods in the shops and online. This makes people want more and more. Not everyone can afford the best houses, holidays, cars, clothes and items for their house. This is the real reason for the high crime rates in capitalist societies like the UK. Poverty also makes people steal because they are desperate for the basics. Therefore, inequality and poverty cause crime.
The forces of social control are in place to protect the property of the bourgeoisie and those with wealth.	Marxists argue that laws are in place to protect property. The agencies of social control are there to make sure that rich people can keep their property. Most effort is put into stopping crime by working-class people. The crimes of the rich are ignored.
The media are also owned by the bourgeoisie (ruling class) and persuade people that the system we live in is fair. They present working-class crime as a big problem for society.	The media report on street crime rather than white-collar and corporate crime. The dramatic news stories about riots, gangs and knife crime are the focus, making people think that these are the real problem. Marxists argue that the scale of white-collar and corporate crime is unknown, but even that which we know about is very harmful to society. The media who promote the interests of the ruling class do not report on these stories.

What is white-collar and corporate crime?

White-collar crime is usually linked to a person's occupation (job) and committed by people from higher social classes. It is for individual gain.	White-collar crime is varied and includes fraud, embezzlement, accepting bribes or other corrupt practices. Individuals take advantage of their position to gain money usually from their employers, but possibly from other individuals.
White-collar crime is often not discovered or reported to the police.	White-collar criminals are so called because of the white collar and tie linked to middle-class jobs. They are often not suspected because of their high social position. White-collar workers are often clever, good at concealing their crimes. Even when they are discovered , many companies do not want the bad publicity so will fire them without involving the police. The MPs' expenses scandal is an example of white-collar crime by very high-status individuals. Few were prosecuted but allowed to return the money.
Corporate crime involves crimes that are committed by big businesses. The company benefits although individuals within it may benefit.	involves a range of activities that benefit the business. This includes false advertising, tax evasion, mis-selling pensions or other financial products, insider trading, not following health and safety rules and negligence.
Corporate crime is often not suspected, discovered or even prosecuted when it is. It may involve huge profits.	Big businesses are often not suspected and are able to afford good lawyers to get themselves out of trouble. Sometimes they just sack individuals involved, pay compensation or apologise. Examples of corporate crime are thalidomide, Tesco horsemeat scandal, PPI mis-selling and asbestos. Marxists add that the media does not focus on corporate crime. They would also argue that some of the activities of big companies may not be illegal but should be. Companies like Amazon to find loopholes which means they avoid paying the taxes needed by the UK.

Strengths of the Marxist view that capitalism causes crime are:

Exposes the huge inequalities of capitalism.	Exposes the greed promoted by our system.	Exposes the harm that poverty does to our society.

Weaknesses of the Marxist view that capitalism causes crime are:

Switzerland has low crime rates and is capitalist.	Countries that have tried communism do not have zero crime rates, e.g. Soviet Russia, Cuba.	Blames society. Ignores individual motives for crime.

Strengths of the Marxist view that the real problem is ruling class crime are:

Shows the inequalities of the law and law enforcement.	Holds to account companies that break health and safety rules putting individuals and the environment at risk.	Holds to account huge companies who make billions across the globe.

Weaknesses of the Marxist view that the real problem is ruling class crime are:

Blames biased policing for high rates of working-class and ethnic minority crime. Functionalists would say that social order needs to be kept.	It ignores the fact that the working class, ethnic minorities and women actually suffer as victims of crime.	Corporate crime is being taken more seriously. Amazon have received a lot of pressure about tax evasion. Other stories like the Alton Towers rollercoaster crash receive lots of publicity.

Strengths of Chambliss's study of crime in Seattle are:

He showed how powerful people were the real criminals in 1970s Seattle in the USA. Exposed corruption in many areas of Seattle life.	The study was done over a whole decade and used interviews with people ranging from lawyers and police to prostitutes.	Showed how the law was not enforced fairly. This is called differential enforcement of the law.

Weaknesses of Chambliss's study of crime in Seattle are:

His study is dated.	Seattle may not be like other cities or the UK.	The study was based on interviews. Chambliss may have asked leading questions. It is difficult to know whether people were truthful.

Marxists see the capitalist rich in control of many areas of society. Which areas can you see in the picture?

Knowledge check

1. Identify two types of white-collar crime. **(2 marks)**
2. Outline what is meant by 'corporate crime'. **(4 marks)**
3. Give reasons why crimes committed by the ruling class are less likely to be prosecuted. **(4 marks)**

Spec spotlight

6.4 Sociological theories and explanations of deviance and criminal behaviour: interactionism, notion of the typical offender, labelling, self-fulfilling prophecy, Becker, deviant career, moral panics

Link to textbook

pp 218–219: What do interactionists contribute to the study of crime?

pp 220–221: The media and crime

AO2 Apply

Find out about the #MeToo campaign. How is this an example of a moral panic?

Take it further

What other examples of moral panics have you noticed in recent times?

People have an idea of what the typical offender will look like. This is often based on stereotypes.

Interactionism

Interactionists try to explain what happens in small-scale, everyday situations.	Unlike Marxists and functionalists, interactionists do not try to explain the whole of society. They are interested in studying small-scale social situations. They often use qualitative methods of research to understand the meanings and motives of individuals.
Interactionists are interested in how people are influenced by the way that other people treat them.	As far as crime is concerned, interactionists say that there is no such thing as a typical offender. People have an idea which is based on stereotypes. The notion of the typical offender is often male, underclass/working class, young and/or ethnic minority. The idea of the typical offender may lead to labelling.
Interactionists believe that the way other people react to us has a powerful effect on our view of ourselves. No actions are criminal or deviant. It is the reaction of others that decide this.	The idea of labelling is one of the most well-known ideas of interactionism. The judgements we make about other people are labels that we use to decide what people are like. The main difference between criminals and ordinary people, according to interactionists, is the fact that they have been labelled as criminal. Most people have broken a law, but most of us have not been caught or convicted.
Interactionists believe that our view of ourselves has an effect on our future behaviour.	These labels have a very powerful effect on people's behaviour. If someone believes that people think they are a thief, murderer or unpleasant this may have an impact on how they see themselves (self-concept) and how they act. They may act out what other people think of them. The way that people live up to their labels is known as a self-fulfilling prophecy.

Interactionism, crime and deviance

Labelling was developed by Howard Becker who also added the idea of the deviant career.	Becker noticed that people that were labelled as deviants or criminals were then likely to follow a deviant career. The deviant career is a process that a person follows when they are labelled. For example, a thief's deviant career could involve: being caught; being branded a thief; other people notice this; more accusations when something goes missing; charged; convicted; labelled as no good by a judge/magistrate; prison; more labelling by others as an ex-convict; more accusations; acceptance of the label of thief; more theft.
Some labels are very powerful and affect the way a person is seen by others.	The label of thief is powerful, but there are others which may be even more unpleasant, e.g. paedophile, rapist, murderer. These labels are very hard to remove and may shape the way a person is seen by others. Interactionists call such labels a 'master status'.
Interactionism has had a great effect on the study of media. Moral panics is a key idea to come from this.	The idea of the moral panic was developed by Stanley Cohen in his book *Folk Devils and Moral Panics* (1972). Moral panics are created by the media who react to an event in the news. They report and sensationalise a crime and often link the crime to a group. The mods and rockers in Cohen's study were labelled as a 'bad' group by the media. The act of labelling them encourages the group to accept its label as bad and live up to this label. Cohen said that these groups become 'folk devils'.
Deviancy amplification is another major contribution of Interactionism.	Interactionists have noticed the way that reactions of the agencies of social control can make crime worse. If the police and media give publicity to criminal or deviant behaviour, they can actually encourage more people to take part. Terrorism is a classic example of this. They thrive on publicity. When crime is made worse in this way, interactionists call it deviancy amplification.

Strengths of the interactionist view of crime and deviance are:

Interactionists have been very good at investigating groups that are not well understood and on the edges of society, e.g. criminals, drug addicts, sub-cultures.	Shows how important the way people treat each other is. Sees humans as active and creative.	Labelling, self-fulfilling prophecy and moral panics and other good ideas have developed from interactionism.

Weaknesses of the interactionist view of crime and deviance are:

Difficult to test the theory.	Does not really explain anything fully. Only explains certain situations, such as classrooms.	They don't really explain why people commit crime in the first place.

Strengths of the theory of labelling are:

It is a useful theory that can improve the way people treat each other.	Shows the harm that labels can do.	Helps us understand small-scale interaction.

Weaknesses of the theory of labelling are:

Makes excuses and takes the blame off the criminal.	Individuals do not always live up to their label, e.g. a teacher may label a student as 'not very bright' and they may react to this by working harder and so rejecting the label.	Does not explain power. Which people have the power to label and why?

Strengths of the theory of moral panics are:

Shows the police that they need to be careful how they react to moral panics.	The theory has been used in many studies, e.g. Sarah Thornton and Marxists such as Stuart Hall.	It is a useful theory that helps us understand the dangers of media reporting.

Weaknesses of the theory of moral panics are:

The media and police cannot just ignore problems.	Some moral panics are serious and justified, e.g. #MeToo campaign.	Cohen does not explain what caused the behaviour in the first place.

Key figure

Edwin M. Lemert investigated stuttering in Native Americans. The Native American groups on the Pacific coastline had no stuttering at all. These tribes had no tradition of public speaking, so no one worried about it.

However, one tribe he studied viewed public speaking as really important. If a child had any speech defect parents reacted with shock and horror. Parents labelled their children as being poor at public speaking. This would cause children to worry about any stuttering or speech defect. In this tribe, stuttering was quite common. Lemert says that this tribe showed the effect that being labelled by their parents had upon the children.

Think link

This topic links closely to education in particular. Labelling is a very useful theory for understanding and improving what happens in a classroom. Interactionists' idea of labelling is well known to all teachers and may prevent this from happening.

Interactionists note how the reactions of others can affect how we see ourselves and how we act in future. Being labelled as criminal or deviant can make people more likely to act in that way.

Knowledge check

1. Identify two labels that could be used to suggest 'criminal'. **(2 marks)**
2. What is the self-fulfilling prophecy? **(4 marks)**
3. Give two reasons why there is a notion of a typical offender. **(4 marks)**
4. 'An important cause of crime is labelling.' Do you agree? **(15 marks)**

Spec spotlight

6.3 Patterns of criminal and deviant behaviour: patterns of criminal behaviour by gender

6.4 Sociological theories and explanations of deviance and criminal behaviour: conflict view of Feminism; social control, Heidensohn and female conformity, women and poverty including the work of Carlen, chivalry thesis

Link to textbook

pp 222–223: How does social control affect levels of female crime and deviance?

pp 224–225: How does poverty affect female crime and deviance?

pp 226–227: Are females treated fairly by the forces of social control

AO2 Apply

A newspaper article says that crime committed by females is on the increase. Explain why this could be happening using sociological terms.

Take it further

Find out whether female crime is on the increase or not in the last few years.

Stereotypes of the typical offender are usually male. Women are associated with certain crimes such as shoplifting.

Feminism

Women are far less likely to be arrested or convicted compared to men.	Crime statistics show that men are committing more crimes than women. There is a large difference between the numbers of males in prison compared to females. Only 5 per cent of prisoners in the UK in 2017 were female.
Women are more likely to be victims of certain crimes than men, particularly domestic abuse and sexual assault or harassment.	Women are more likely to be convicted of certain crimes including shoplifting but overall their offending rates are much lower. Men are more likely to be victims of an assault than women.
The way girls are socialised is believed to be a main reason for lower rates of female crime.	Traditional gender roles have socialised girls to be quiet and gentle. This type of personality does not fit with crime. On the other hand boys may be socialised to be tough, aggressive and to be risk takers, which behaviours are more likely to result in crime.
Women are also more closely controlled from childhood and even when they are adults.	Girls are not allowed as much freedom as boys to 'protect' themselves. Even as women they are subject to greater social control. For instance, women who do not conform to norms of being a 'good' woman may be sanctioned through the fear of gossip or name calling. This keeps many women in check.

Sociological concepts, gender and crime

Women were ignored by many criminologists. Otto Pollak was one of the first to develop ideas about female crime.	Pollak developed the 'chivalry thesis', which is the idea that women are not punished as harshly by the agents of social control from teachers to judges and the police who feel sorry for women who get into trouble and go easy on them. This accounts for all the extra men in prison, according to this view.
Frances Heidensohn developed the idea that women live in a male-controlled world and must conform to society's expectations.	According to Heidensohn, we live in a patriarchy and women have to behave according to the norms of their role. Women get less opportunity because they have fewer opportunities to commit crime as there is such great social control over them.
A different view is that of the demonisation of women.	This view states that women are treated more harshly by the forces of social control for certain crimes. Women who commit crimes which do not fit with ideas about how a women or mother should behave are treated especially harshly by the media. They are demonised for crimes involving any aspect of cruelty in a way that a man would not be.
Violent crime is linked closely to men.	This is often linked to ideas about masculinity. Men are expected to be aggressive and tough and violence can fit with this. The crisis of masculinity may mean that some men need to 'prove' their masculinity in other ways even more if they cannot prove it through being a breadwinner.

Strengths of the chivalry thesis are:

There are much greater numbers of male arrests, convictions and a vastly greater percentage of men are in prison.

The thesis may not be completely true, yet it was an important study as it started off the study of female crime. Even though it was written by a man it was a step forward and started the debate.

The view of different treatment of boys at school traditionally may have some merit. Women may also be treated more leniently if they are pregnant or already mothers.

Weaknesses of the chivalry thesis are:

The original study by Pollak was not based on evidence.

It acts as an excuse for male crime and tries to say that men are not as guilty as it appears.

Pollak's view that women were better at hiding their crimes was not really backed up with any evidence for this and just suited his theory.

Strengths of the theory of the demonisation of women are:

This theory challenges the chivalry thesis. Women are treated worse than men, especially by the media, if they are guilty of some crimes.

There are lots of examples of the demonisation of women in the media. Myra Hindley, Rose West and Maxine Carr are examples of this.

Pat Carlen suggests that courts treat women worse if they do not fit the gender stereotype of good mother and housewife.

Weaknesses of the theory of the demonisation of women are:

The cases where women are demonised are extreme cases.

Lower numbers of females in prisons may suggest that women are less likely to be convicted and sent to prison.

Men who commit crimes involving cruelty are also demonised. However, there are fewer women involved in such crimes.

Sociologists say that there has been a crisis of masculinity for young men who are shut out from their traditional role of breadwinner. There has also been a decline in traditional masculine manual jobs.

REVISION BOOSTER

Answers to questions on gender and crime often only refer to women. Refer to evidence, studies and histories of men as well as women.

Key figure

Pat Carlen is an essential figure to know; she tried to explain why some women do turn to crime. Women are more likely to live in poverty for a variety of reasons including low pay and being a single parent.

Carlen interviewed and observed a group of 39 women aged between 15 and 46. Her research was qualitative, and she found that crime had a range of meanings for women. Some turned to crime for excitement and others because of problems they had with drugs and alcohol.

Think link

This topic links closely to stratification and life-chances. It also links to the family and ideas about traditional gender roles.

Knowledge check

1. Identify two ways in which social control may be stricter for females. **(2 marks)**
2. 'Females are treated less harshly by the police and courts.' Do you agree? **(15 marks)**

Spec spotlight

6.3 Patterns of criminal and deviant behaviour: patterns of criminal behaviour by ethnicity

6.4 Sociological theories and explanations of deviance and criminal behaviour: ethnicity and crime, racism, institutional racism, scapegoating

Link to textbook

pp 228–229: What is the situation for ethnic minorities and crime?

pp 230–231: Institutional racism

AO2 Apply

The Ministry of Justice produced a report in 2017 stating that about 9 in every 10,000 young black people were locked up in secure units such as young offender institutions. For white young people it was 1 in 10,000.

What sociological explanations can you apply to these figures?

Take it further →

What other questions about the above figures would you like to know the answers to?

Institutional racism

Ethnicity is the cultural group to which a person belongs.	Some ethnic groups have higher arrest and conviction rates than others. African-Caribbean males are over-represented in the crime statistics. People from ethnic minority groups also are more likely to be victims of crime. Hate crime has doubled in the UK since the Brexit vote in 2016.
Higher conviction rates for some ethnic minorities may be based on harmful stereotypes and assumptions about black people.	The attitudes of police officers and courts have been linked to these stereotypes. Sociologists have written about the idea of a 'canteen culture' for police officers which is racist and sexist.
The Stephen Lawrence case is famous because it brought to light racist attitudes in the police force.	Stephen Lawrence was a black teenager murdered by racists whose case was not investigated effectively by the police. The reason for this was found to be racist assumptions made by the officers. The Macpherson Report which followed found the police to be institutionally racist. Racism was found deep within the culture of the police.
The Stephen Lawrence case has prompted the police to spend time training recruits to have greater awareness of stereotyping and discrimination.	Despite the efforts to improve, the police in the UK were embarrassed by a report written by human rights experts for the United Nations. In April 2018, they released a report 25 years on from Stephen's death criticising the UK police. They said that black people were more likely to die in custody and that ethnic minorities were overpoliced and criminalised in the UK.

Studies based on ethnicity and crime

The high levels of convictions for ethnic minority groups has led to different viewpoints.	One view is that poverty is closely linked to high levels of crime. Some ethnic minority groups are more likely to live in poverty and therefore may turn to crime. The New Right would argue that the culture of poverty leads to crime and that ethnic minorities are more likely to live in poverty.
Other famous studies were completed by Paul Gilroy.	Gilroy has been criticised for saying that on one hand there is not as much ethnic minority crime as the figures say because the police are racist. At the same time, he says that there is a lot of ethnic minority crime because of racism. However, Gilroy's work raises questions about official statistics.
Ethnic minority groups are often the focus of moral panics and receive negative attention because of this.	Islamophobia has been a feature of the reporting in the press in recent years. The threat from Islamic terrorism may be used to create stereotypes about all Asians. *The Independent* in 2017 claimed that the *Daily Mail*, the *Sun* and the *Daily Express* all published inaccurate stories about Asians, causing hostility. Stuart Hall found that black people were stereotyped as muggers in the 1970s.

Bowling and Phillips found that ethnic minority defendants often decided to go to Crown Court, where a jury would try them, as they were mistrustful of magistrates.

Strengths of the view that the extent of ethnic minority crime is caused by stereotypes are:

Stereotypes held by agents of social control, such as the police and courts, may lead to labelling and a self-fulfilling prophecy for some individuals from ethnic minorities.

Studies by Gilroy and Hall support the view that stereotypes of ethnic minorities are common in society. Agencies of socialisation, such as the media, schools and the police may all be influenced by these views.

The Macpherson Report was sponsored by the government. The report found that it was not the fault of individual officers but the whole organisation, which had a pattern of processes and thinking based on thoughtlessness, ignorance and prejudice. There are still concerns about this.

Weaknesses of the view that the extent of ethnic minority crime is caused by stereotypes are:

Entry to the police has become more difficult and the police are becoming better educated at dealing with ethnic minority groups.

There may be other causes of higher rates of ethnic minority crime. Some ethnic minority groups are more likely to be living in poverty, which is itself more closely linked to crime.

The New Right argue that there is a culture of poverty which includes crime as a social norm. Ethnic minorities are likely to be involved in crime if they live in poverty.

Strengths of the view that the forces of social control continue to treat ethnic minorities unfairly are:

A UN Report in 2018 found that black people were three times more likely to be tasered than white people.

Exclusion rates from school are higher for some ethnic minority groups.

In 2018, David Lammy MP produced a review which showed that black people were more likely to be sent to prison in the UK than the USA.

The Windrush scandal (2018) has resulted in unfair treatment of many people who had a right to British citizenship. The harsh treatment received through the home office shows how the 'hostile environment' policy made life unfair for some British citizens based on their ethnicity.

Weaknesses of the view that the forces of social control continue to treat ethnic minorities unfairly are:

Stephen Lawrence's murder led to the creation of the Independent Police Complaints Commission.

Make use of the words in this image in a discussion about racism in the UK.

Between 2007 and 2018 , the percentage of police officers from ethnic minority groups increased from 3.9 per cent to 6.6 per cent. This is a significant step forward and recruitment targets are higher still. Fourteen per cent of the population as a whole come from ethnic minority groups.

It is difficult to discount the evidence that ethnic minorities receive harsher treatment, but awareness has been raised since Stephen Lawrence and efforts are being made to improve things. There are a number of organisations, such as the Runnymede Trust, which are having success with projects to improve the rights of ethnic minority groups.

Key figures

Ben Bowling and Coretta Phillips published a study in 2002 (*Racism, Crime and Justice*) which had interesting findings. They found that cases against ethnic minority individuals were more likely to be dropped by the Crown Prosecution Service than those against white people. They argue that this is because the initial cases were based on stereotyping against ethnic minorities instead of evidence.

Think link

When answering a question about ethnicity, remember to consider whether gender, social class or age may be a factor. Consider this when looking at the AO2 Apply section on this page.

Knowledge check

1. Describe what is meant by 'institutional racism'. **(4 marks)**
2. Explain why some ethnic minority groups have higher conviction rates. **(8 marks)**

Spec spotlight

6.3 Patterns of criminal and deviant behaviour: patterns of criminal behaviour by social class, ethnicity, age, gender

6.5 Sources of data on crime: patterns and trends of criminal behaviour

Link to textbook

AO2 Apply

The Age Crime Curve is accepted by many as a well-established pattern. What sociological explanations can you think of for the rise in crime amongst teenagers, dropping off once they reach their early twenties? Can you explain why it begins to reduce after this? Include as many sociological terms as you can.

Take it further

How does a moral panic affect the patterns of crime?

Identify two patterns of crime in the UK today.

Patterns of crime

Some people believe that there was a 'golden age' in the past where crime rates were much lower in the UK.	In fact, since Tony Blair's Labour government was elected in 1997, crime rates in official statistics have gone down. However, it is hard to judge comparative crime rates over time. For example, there are lots of new crimes that did not exist in 1997, due to new technology.
Conviction rates are much higher for the working class than other groups.	It is difficult to set this apart from gender and age. There is a huge gender gap still in convictions and younger people are much more likely to be convicted than older people. Therefore, working-class males are more likely to be arrested and convicted. To add further complexity some ethnic minority groups are much more likely to be arrested and convicted.
The age crime curve is accepted by most criminologists.	The age crime curve sees more crime committed by people during their teenage years and increasing into their early twenties and then beginning to reduce.
The National Crime Survey for the year ending June 2018 showed an increase in the homicide rate and a rise in theft and burglary. Overall crime rates were stable, although computer misuse had gone down by 30 per cent.	The *Guardian* newspaper reported in April 2018 a surge in gun and knife crime, as well as homicides. In London this was greater than in other parts of the country. There is some concern that this is coupled with cuts in police numbers.

Victimisation

Some groups are more likely to be victims of crime than other groups.	Hate crime has been on the rise since the Brexit vote. Hate crimes are linked to racism, homophobia and prejudice against disabled people.
14 per cent of people in England and Wales were victims of crime in 2016–17.	A higher percentage of people from some ethnic minority groups, including black and mixed race, were victims of crime compared to white people.
People living in poverty are more likely to be victims of crime. This would include the working class as well as the unemployed.	Figures from the Office for National Statistics in 2018 show that young people aged 16–24 years old are more likely to be a victim of crime than older people. White men were more likely to be victim of crime than white women.
The Crime Survey for England and Wales is one of the most important sources of data on crime.	Full Fact is an independent charity which checks facts independently. They agree that crime as reported by adults has been falling since the mid 1990s. However, some crimes have been going up. Violent crime and sexual crime are examples of this. The rise may be because people are more confident about reporting crime.

Strengths of the view that there was a golden age when there was less crime are:

Many crimes that now exist were not around then, such as cyber crime. It is difficult to judge, but violent crime has seen some increases in recent years.

The population has increased in the last 100 years and cities are busier and more anonymous than ever. Places may previously have felt safer. This may be a significant change in the feel of our cities and towns.

Charles Murray, a New Right sociologist, argues that crime has become worse in the USA and UK because of the welfare state. Benefits have meant a decline in marriage and an increase in lone parents. The strength of the nuclear family in the past may have meant less crime.

Weaknesses of the view that there was a golden age when there was less crime are:

The view that a golden age existed sometime in the past is not a new idea. Successive generations have made this out to be the case.

The media exaggerate and create moral panics about the extent of crime. They sensationalise extreme crime.

Geoffrey Pearson's study *Hooligan* shows that there were menaces on Britain's streets even in Victorian times. Footpads and hooligans were around even then.

Strengths of the view that crime has decreased since the mid 1990s are:

The National Crime Survey for England and Wales has continued to show decreases in crime.

Even where certain crimes have increased reporting, this may simply be due to an increased confidence to report crime by the public.

Crime figures have decreased even though mobile phones have made reporting crime even easier.

Weaknesses of the view that crime has decreased since the mid 1990s are:

Certain crimes have been increasing. There is a fear that knives and guns are appearing on Britain's streets more often.

Official statistics are open to question as shown in the next spread.

The police and government are under pressure to reduce crime figures and may try to reduce the statistics.

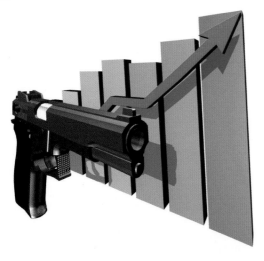

Many headlines in the UK feature stories about an increase in gun and knife crime. Do the statistics support this view?

Knowledge check

1. Identify two patterns of crime in the UK today. (4 marks)
2. 'Crime is becoming worse in the UK.' Do you agree with this statement? (15 marks)

Spec spotlight

6.5 Sources of data on crime: official statistics, victim and self-report studies, usefulness of sources of data on crime, dark figure of crime, unreported and unrecorded crime, police bias and labelling, moral panics, invisible crime

Link to textbook

AO2 Apply

The BBC reported in 2017 that knife crime had risen by 22 per cent in 2017. Firearms offences also increased by 11 per cent. Other crimes had not increased.

What explanations can you give for the rise? Include as many sociological ideas as you can.

Take it further

Criminology experts have suggested using Twitter and social media to track the extent of crime. What advantages and disadvantages would this have?

Official statistics and crime

The main survey for crime in the UK is the Crime Survey for England and Wales. This is collected annually and published by the Office for National Statistics.	Crime statistics have normally been based upon reported and recorded crime in the UK. There are many reasons why these statistics may be called into question. There are many reasons why a crime may never be reported, let alone recorded.
Victim surveys are also used to improve the quality of data collected by the government.	Victim surveys involve people completing a survey to ask them whether they have been a victim of crime. This has resulted in a more accurate picture of crime. The Crime Survey for England and Wales is a victim survey. The government believes this is more accurate than police figures as it includes non-reported crime.
Self-report studies are an alternative method collected by some social researchers.	Self-report studies involve respondents anonymously admitting whether they have committed crimes in the past. This adds a more complete picture of crime in the UK.
The aim of collecting official statistics is so that the government can understand what is happening in society.	The government can use the information to decide on where to use resources to tackle crime. It also helps voters to decide whether they think the government is doing a good job or not. This puts pressure on the government to deliver improving figures. It also puts pressure on the police to supply these.

Problems with official statistics on crime

Not all crime is reported by the public.	There are many reasons for crime not being reported. This includes embarrassment, thinking the crime is too small, fear of reprisals or knowing the perpetrator. Sexual assault may not be reported due to embarrassment, fear or shame. On the other hand, people are more likely to report some crimes. For instance, car crime may be reported in order to claim insurance.
The police may not record all crimes.	There is pressure on the police to keep crime figures down. The process of No Criming has featured in the press recently. The police make a decision that a crime has not happened and this does not feature in the statistics. Police also decide how to record crimes. Are five burglaries in one night in a street five crimes or one? Different forces may record in different ways.
There are lots of changes in the way that official statistics are recorded.	New crimes are created by changes in the law or new technology. Certain issues are highlighted by the media and this makes people more likely to report that crime. The #MeToo campaign is an example of this.
The media play a large role in creating public awareness of different crimes.	Some sociologists such as Stanley Cohen argue that moral panics are created by the media. This results in deviancy amplification. More people are likely to commit the offence, be aware of the offence and the offence is more likely to be investigated by the police. This will affect the official statistics.

Embezzlement and corruption are all examples of white-collar crime. They are unlikely to appear in official statistics as many of those involved are not suspected, charged or convicted.

Strengths of the view that official statistics on crime can be trusted by sociologists are:		
Statistics have been collected in a systematic way over many years. It is possible to make comparisons over time. Results are large scale.	The police are a professional organisation and have to keep careful records. They have been well trained.	The government has acted to increase the accuracy of official statistics on crime by making Victim Reports a key part of the Crime Survey for England and Wales.
The government claims that figures from the Crime Survey for England and Wales are the most accurate available.	Official statistics are public and open to criticism. This has meant that they are carefully collected. All crimes are given a crime number.	It is very easy to criticise official statistics on crime, but we cannot just give up because of this. There has to be an attempt to gather statistics and they do give us an idea of shifting patterns of crime.

Weaknesses of the view that official statistics on crime can be trusted by sociologists are:		
Some crimes are never reported by the public for a variety of reasons. Therefore, the official statistics can never be accurate.	There is a hidden or dark figure of crime that is never known by the police or the government. Many crimes lie beneath the surface and remain unknown.	The police have changed their methods of recording crime many times over the years. There is also pressure on the police to keep figures low and to have a good clear-up rate for crime. People may report crimes more often if they are confident that they will be listened to.
Styles of policing may affect the statistics. Zero tolerance policing will result in a high number of arrests and convictions.	Institutional racism will also affect statistics. Stop and search figures for ethnic minority groups are higher than for other groups resulting in more arrests.	Police bias to other groups may result in labelling and more arrests of certain groups.
Marxists argue that working-class crime (street crime or blue-collar crime) is the focus of the police resulting in more arrests. This is called selective law enforcement.	Marxists also say that white-collar crime and corporate crime are not likely to be a focus for the police. These criminals are able to avoid detection and conviction. Expensive lawyers will get them out of trouble.	Invisible crime may happen and some people are not even aware a crime has taken place. This adds to the crime below the surface. Examples of this are vandalism and pollution.
Pollak's chivalry thesis may mean that there are fewer females arrested due to more lenient treatment of females by those in authority.	Pat Carlen's study suggests the courts may be harder on women who do not match stereotypes about being a good mother.	Moral panics will influence the number of crimes committed or dealt with by the police. People will copy crimes that there are moral panics about. The police are more likely to clamp down on these.

The #MeToo campaign has encouraged many women around the world to come forward reporting historical sexual harassment. What impact would this have on official statistics of crime?

REVISION BOOSTER

There are lots of reasons for the lack of trust in official statistics. Some of these are theoretical and some are more practical. Make sure that you have examples to back them up which will breathe life into your answer.

Think link

This spread links to work on Research Methods. Official statistics on crime are a form of secondary data. Sociologists that use them in their work need to remember that they have been collected by other people who have their own reasons for doing so and their own goals. For instance, the government wishes to look as though it is winning the war on crime.

Key figure

Dick Hobbs' book *Doing the Business* (1989) is an interesting study of the East End of London. He found that working-class criminals and police had a unique way of dealing with each other. Arrest and sharing of information was like a game played between criminals and police. Negotiation and deals were part of this. If Hobbs' view is true then it calls into question official statistics collected by the police.

Knowledge check

1. Describe what is meant by 'official statistics on crime'.

   (4 marks)

2. Explain why sociologists are cautious about the use of official statistics on crime.

   (8 marks)

Spec spotlight

6.4 Sociological theories and explanations of deviance and criminal behaviour (structural, subcultural, interactionist and feminist)

Link to textbook

pp 186–237: This spread draws together threads from across the whole of Chapter 5 Crime and deviance

AO2 Apply

There are a lot of theories of crime; more than we can cover here. Do not lose sight of some of the earlier topics that you studied. Apply the following terms to ideas about the causes of crime:

- *norms and values*
- *socialisation*
- *gender roles*
- *nature versus nurture debate*
- *informal and formal social control.*

This will be good revision for Chapter 1 Key concepts and processes of cultural transmission as well as Chapter 5 Crime and deviance.

Take it further

Find studies from Chapter 2 Families and Chapter 3 Education which you could link to crime.

Television is the leading cause of violence in today's society:
☐ Agree
☐ Disagree

Television has been blamed for violence increasing in society. The argument is that people imitate what they see on television and that people become desensitised to the effects of violence. What role could other media play in causing violence?

Functionalist, subcultural and structural theories of the causes of crime

Functionalists like Emile Durkheim see crime as a natural part of society.	Durkheim saw crime as a result of anomie. Anomie means normlessness. The unwritten rules that keep society in order have been forgotten and society gets out of control. The riots in the UK in 2011 would be a good example of this.
Robert K. Merton explained crime through the idea of strain theory.	Merton was an American who believed that the power of the American Dream made people want success so badly that they were prepared to use crime to get it. Not everyone turned to crime and some individuals carried on normally, others gave up, some turned to drugs or drink and others rebelled against society. Merton, a functionalist, explained a range of criminal and deviant behaviour through strain theory.
Albert Cohen criticised Merton as his theory does not explain crimes that are not committed for money.	Cohen developed a subcultural theory which explained how groups turn to crime. Some groups experience status frustration as they are unable to be successful through honest means. These groups form a subculture that turns everyday norms and values upside down.
Charles Murray, a New Right sociologist, argued that the subculture of the poor was a key cause of crime.	Murray called the subculture of the poor the culture of poverty. Low aspirations, spending on benefits and crime are a part of this way of life.

Marxist, interactionist and feminist views of the causes of crime

Marxism blames crime on society. In particular, they see capitalism as creating an unfair society.	On one hand, Marxists see some crime as a result of poverty. It is not surprising that people steal when they are surrounded by advertisements for expensive goods. However, they also argue that the ruling class control the police and the courts to keep the working class under control. Corporate crime is ignored by the forces of social control.
Interactionists have given some very interesting ideas to the sociology of crime. Labelling and moral panics are two of these.	Interactionists use labelling to explain how a criminal may follow a deviant career. The criminal is labelled after committing one crime and finds the label difficult to live with. This results in a self-fulfilling prophecy.
Moral panics have also been a major contribution of interactionism.	Stanley Cohen introduced the idea in his book *Folk Devils and Moral Panics* where he studied the process of a moral panic. He used the example of the Mods and Rockers in the 1960s. He showed how one incident was sensationalised and blown out of proportion by the media. This resulted in a moral panic and the mods and rockers were made into folk devils. This had the result of making the crime and deviance worse (deviancy amplification).
Feminists have explained reasons for female crime.	Pat Carlen explained crime of women as a matter of choice for a variety of reasons. Other feminists like Frances Heidensohn explained lower rates of female crime as a result of greater social control over females. Some sociologists have suggested that the study of why females commit less crime may help to reduce male crime.

Strengths of the idea that anomie is the main cause of crime are:

Anomie explains situations when law and order breaks down. It makes sense when understanding people's behaviour in a riot. It shows how important norms are.

The idea of anomie gives a society ideas on how to restore order. For instance, a school with bad behaviour will try to establish new norms of how to behave, possibly by issuing a new uniform, new rewards and rules.

Shows how fast social change can damage society.

Weaknesses of the idea that anomie is the main cause of crime are:

Blames it on society going wrong, not the individual who commits crime.

Does not consider the power of the ruling class to blame crime on the poor.

Ignores crimes by the wealthy and powerful. Does not really explain why they want even more wealth.

Strengths of Marxist views on the causes of crime are:

Marxism shows the effect that capitalism has upon people. Consumerism is making people selfish and unhappy.

Marxism exposes the crimes of the rich and powerful.

Marxism shows the unfairness of the police and media focus on working-class crime.

Weaknesses of Marxist views on the causes of crime are:

It is not true anymore to say that corporate crime and higher social class crime is ignored. There have been many high-profile cases which have had a lot of media attention, e.g. phone hacking, MPs' expenses scandal. Some MP's were prosecuted.

Ignores gender and ethnicity. Social class is part of the explanation of crime, but gender and ethnicity are also needed for a full explanation.

Ignores the fact that working-class people suffer from crime committed by other working-class people. Of course, the police have to stop this.

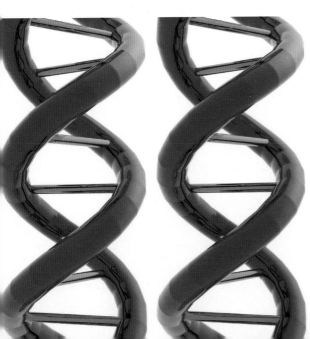

The nature argument is that criminals have different genes that make it more likely that they will engage in crime. Hans Eysenck believed that people had a tendency to be either extrovert or introvert. Extroverts take more risks and crave excitement and are more likely to commit crime. Sociologists would see socialisation as a much greater cause of crime than genes or personality type.

REVISION BOOSTER

There are a lot of different theories about crime which can be very confusing. It is useful to revise them by splitting them into categories based on theories. This will also help you to organise your theories.

Think link

This spread should help you link together all of the work that you have completed on crime and deviance. In addition, there are important links back to Chapter 1: Key concepts and processes of cultural transmission.

Key figure

Travis Hirschi argued that crime happens when a person's bonds to society are weak. There are four types of bond: attachment, commitment, belief and involvement. With this viewpoint, a person would be likely to turn to crime and deviance if they had weak family links, did not attend school, had little hopes for the future or career plan. They would not take part in clubs or feel a positive connection to society. Hirschi's theory is called 'Control Theory'.

Marxists criticise the theory as it blames individuals when the problem is society not involving the person. It also ignores pull factors such as peer pressure.

Knowledge check

1. Outline what is meant by a 'criminal subculture'. **(4 marks)**
2. Discuss the main causes of crime in 21st-century UK.
   (15 marks)

Spec spotlight

4.1 Usefulness of different types of data: primary and secondary data, quantitative and qualitative data, sources of secondary data, usefulness of these types of data to sociologists

Link to textbook
pp 240–241: Different types of research and data
pp 248–249: Secondary data

AO2 Apply

Explain how the record books of a charity such as a food bank could be useful to a sociologist.

Explain how the stories and reports that primary school children write about their 'news' could be used by sociologists.

The census is collected every ten years in the UK. It records the basic details and population count of every household. This is one of the most important sets of official statistics collected and a useful source of information.

Primary data

Data is the information that sociologists base their ideas on.	Primary data means research information that sociologists have collected themselves. There is a range of methods used by sociologists to collect information.
Common methods linked to sociology.	In fact, survey is a very general term which is used to describe a research project which may use a variety of methods. When you write about research methods you need to be more specific.
Primary data may include questionnaires, interviews, observation and even experiments.	There are lots of different styles of all of these methods. All have their advantages and disadvantages. Sociologists do not often use experiments because people do not act naturally in what is an unrealistic situation. Therefore, the results are not valid.
Data can also be split into two main types: quantitative and qualitative.	Quantitative data provides statistics, percentages and graphs etc, (i.e. quantities). Qualitative data has more detail and description, for example, a survey or questionnaire.

Secondary data

Secondary data means data that was not collected by the sociologists themselves.	Sociologists make use of all kinds of data that people have collected for other purposes. This can include novels, diaries, official statistics, newspapers, films, television and radio. In modern times, social media, blogs and other information found on the Internet could be used.
Secondary data may be quantitative or qualitative.	Sociologists have to be careful when using secondary data. They should always remember that the information was collected for a different purpose.
Secondary data may come in very different forms.	The different ways that data was collected may make it difficult to compare data from different people or organisations.
Qualitative secondary data, such as novels and diaries, can give sociologists important and highly valid information about societies.	Secondary data is a very cheap way of collecting information for sociologists as the information is already there. Quantitative data, such as official statistics on crime or health, can help sociologists spot patterns and trends over time.

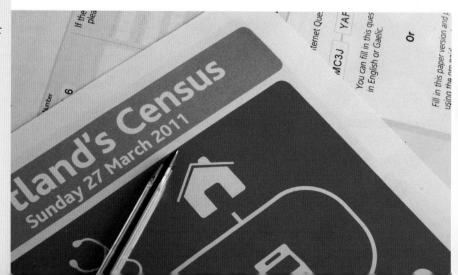

Strengths of qualitative data are:

The information collected is rich in detail and description.	The information is high in validity and may present a true picture of society.	The detailed information may give the sociologist greater understanding and help them create questions for research.

Weaknesses of qualitative data are:

It is time consuming to collect.	Only a small number of people are studied. The sample may not be representative (fair).	Often low in reliability. It is hard to repeat studies that collect qualitative data.

Strengths of quantitative data are:

Large amounts of data can be collected. Easy to get a fair sample.	Patterns can be seen in the data. Statistics and graphs can be created.	High in reliability. The study can be repeated with the same questions allowing a real comparison of different people, groups or areas.

Weaknesses of quantitative data are:

Lacks detail of information.	Links between statistics do not always prove causes. Poverty can be linked to doing badly in education by statistics. Does poverty cause people to fail at education or does failing at education cause poverty?	Low in validity. The sociologist is not able to gain a true picture of society.

Strengths of secondary data are:

Cheap and easy source of quantitative data.	Qualitative data is very useful for understanding societies in the past or different cultures.	Content analysis has been a very useful method to study the media. Tally charts are used to see how often certain things appear in the media.

Weaknesses of secondary data are:

Data is not always in the form needed by the sociologist.	Hard to make comparisons of statistics. The way they are collected changes over time.	The data may have been collected in a biased way by the person or organisation who collected it.

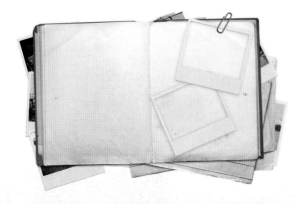

Diaries, journals and photographs are an important source of information about societies in the past. Used by historians, but also by sociologists.

REVISION BOOSTER

Make sure you are aware of the wide range of sources of data used by sociologists. Specific types you may be asked about are listed in the syllabus:

- secondary data: diaries, journals, official and non-official statistics
- primary data: questionnaires, structured and unstructured interviews and different types of observation.

Think link

When you are trying to gain marks for evaluation (Skill AO3) comment on a key study if you know the type of data used. For instance, Paul Willis used qualitative methods in his study of a Wolverhampton secondary school. If his study was repeated in a different school, the results may be very different, meaning his study has low reliability.

Key figure

The **Glasgow University Media Group** is not a single person, but a group who have spent time analysing the content of the media. Their book *Bad News for Refugees* (2013) analyses the content of the media and shows that stories about immigrants are presented in an overwhelmingly negative way and add to harmful stereotypes.

Knowledge check

1. Describe what is meant by 'primary data'. **(2 marks)**
2. Explain two reasons why secondary data is useful for sociologists. **(4 marks)**
3. Discuss the usefulness of quantitative data for the study of behaviour at school. **(6 marks)**

Spec spotlight

4.2 Methods of research: questionnaires, the value, practical application and strength of different methods in terms of validity, reliability, ethics, representativeness

Link to textbook

pp 242–243: How useful are questionnaires in social research?

AO2 Apply

Design a short questionnaire with around five questions on a sociological topic. For example, 'Is crime getting worse?' or "Why are girls achieving better exam results than boys?".

Think about the considerations on this page when designing your questions.

Take it further

Identify the problems with these questions.

- What problems did you have when you were growing up in your family?
- Have you started drinking alcohol yet?
- How often have you lived in poverty?
- Have you experienced people being prejudiced towards you?
- What do you think of the prime minister?

Questionnaires

Questionnaires are one of the most well-known and popular research methods used by sociologists.	Questionnaires include a list of pre-set questions answered by a respondent. Sometimes questionnaires are completed by hand, sometimes online. They can be self-completion or completed by an interviewer.
Questionnaires may include both open and closed questions.	Closed questions have fixed responses which allow the collection of statistics. They may use multiple-choice style responses. This helps sociologists see patterns in the data collected. They also allow large amounts of data to be collected from a large sample of people. Open questions can allow more detailed responses.
Self-completion questionnaires make research very quick and cheap.	Interviewers can help overcome some of the problems with questionnaires. For instance, people may not understand the questions being asked and an interviewer can clarify the meaning of questions. Unfortunately, an interviewer adds to the cost of the research. Interviewers require pay and training.
Postal questionnaires were used a lot in the past but are now seen as quite a costly method.	Technology has allowed the use of online questionnaires. These allow speedy collation of results and reduce workload dramatically. They are especially useful for closed questions and also allow the presentation of data in the form of graphs and percentage tables.

Considerations when using questionnaires

Questionnaire design is highly skilled and there are many pitfalls to avoid.	One problem may be the use of loaded or leading questions. The use of certain words in the question may prompt the person responding to answer in a certain way. For instance, 'Why do you think that crime is rising?' assumes that the person thinks that crime is going up. Neutral language will also help this issue.
Questionnaires must be very clear and easy for the respondent to complete, especially if is self-completion.	The design should also consider ethical issues such as informed consent. The respondent should understand the purpose of the research and what it will be used for. Will the results be published, and will they have anonymity?
It is often hard for the researcher designing the questions to anticipate the different ways that questions are interpreted.	Sometimes the answers may not tell the researcher what they hoped. A pilot study is the best way to overcome problems in question design. The researcher will pick up problems and be able to revise the questions for the actual study.
Language should be chosen carefully to ensure that all those answering will understand the responses.	Questions should also be short and to the point. Too many questions may put respondents off from completing it. Questions should not be offensive to any person completing the questionnaire.

Closed questions on questionnaires can limit the responses. This may lower the validity of those responses.

Strengths of questionnaires are:

They are a quick and cheap method of collecting lots of data.

The use of consistent questions means that responses can be compared easily. This increases reliability and confidence that any differences between different groups are real. Detailed explanation of the questions means that a different researcher can repeat research years later or in a different place allowing real comparisons.

The speed and low cost of questionnaires will allow a representative sample of a large population like that of the UK to be gathered. This increases representativeness as long as care is taken over sampling.

Weaknesses of questionnaires are:

It is easy for people to give false answers. This causes the research to have lower validity.

The researcher designing the questions may impose their own meanings onto the topic they are studying. Their questions will be influenced by their own views and they may not think of the right questions or answers, especially if responses are multiple choice.

Opened-ended questions may be ignored in the write up of the research. In the desire to create statistics the researcher may ignore them as they are harder to classify. Even if they do include them they may simplify them into categories. This will lower validity.

Strengths of postal questionnaires are:

They allow the researcher to select who they are sending the questionnaires to and which areas.

Respondents are not under pressure and can respond when they have time to respond.

Repeat mailings can be used to make sure everyone replies.

Weaknesses of postal questionnaires are:

Expense. The cost of stamps has become much greater. The researcher will also have to pay for return postage.

Low response rate. People are very busy nowadays and are unlikely to take the time to complete the questionnaire and may forget to post it.

Only a certain kind of person bothers to complete a questionnaire. This may include people who have strong opinions about the topic of the questionnaire. This may affect the representativeness of the sample.

Online surveys have made questionnaires even quicker and cheaper. What problems does this not solve?

REVISION BOOSTER

Questions which require evaluation will make this clear in the action word of the question. This may be 'Discuss' or 'Do you agree?'. Make sure that you present both sides of the debate.

Think link

When asked to choose a research method and justify your choice, it may be useful to consider other methods and explain why the method chosen is more appropriate than others.

Key figure

The **Great British Class Survey** was published in 2013. 160,000 people completed the large-scale survey which can be said to have high reliability. Results showed that more than 50 per cent of the population were middle class at the turn of the century. They calculated this by looking at how many people were working in non-manual occupations. However, some non-manual workers may still see themselves as working class for other reasons than their job, which would make the study lose validity.

Knowledge check

1. Describe what is meant by 'questionnaire'. (2 marks)
2. Identify two types of questionnaire. (2 marks)
3. Discuss the usefulness of questionnaires. (12 marks)

Link to textbook

pp 244–245: How useful are interviews in social research?

AO2 Apply

You have been asked to study teenagers in gangs. What method would you choose? Give reasons for your choice of method.

Take it further

Anticipate problems that you would have in carrying out your research using the method that you have chosen.

Interviews

Interviews are one of the most common forms of research used by sociologists. There are two main types, which are structured and unstructured.

Structured interviews are similar to a questionnaire which is completed with the help of an interviewer. There is a list of standardised questions which may include closed and open questions. The use of standardised questions makes the research more reliable.

Interviewers require a great deal of training as the job is highly skilled. This results in higher costs and more time.

Both styles of interview are first-hand and are able to capture a close up view of reality. This is likely to increase the validity of the research. The interviewer hears the respondent explaining things in their own words.

Unstructured interviews offer an even closer and more detailed exploration of society. The interview is more like a conversation.

The researcher prepares a list of topics for the interview and may pre-plan specific questions. However, the interviews are flexible, and the interviewer may think of more answers as the discussion develops. The interviewer may find out the answers to questions they had not even considered.

Bias is a concern at all stages of the interview process from question design to actually asking the questions.

The way questions are asked may affect the responses gained in the interview. The personal characteristics of the interviewer may also affect the responses gained. Social desirability is one factor which may affect the responses. Respondents have a tendency to give answers which they think the interviewer may expect or hope to hear. This can affect the validity level of research.

Considerations when using interviews

The interviewer needs to decide how to collect the information.

Some interviewers will rely on their memory and write up their results straight afterwards. Others may record the interview or make notes as it progresses. Recording the interview may make the respondent uncomfortable. Making notes may make it difficult to maintain eye contact and establish rapport.

Training interviewers to overcome the problems of social desirability or interview bias.

Interviewers need to be trained to keep expressions neutral when asking questions and listening to answers.

The location of the interviews is an important consideration.

Setting up a location for the interviews which is relaxed may make the respondents more likely to be honest. If interviewing children or young people having snacks and drinks may create a more relaxed interview. This adds to validity.

Planning research is important. Interviews may be more difficult than thought.

A pilot study is a good idea to iron out any problems and improve questions. This is very important for a structured interview and may change the direction of research using unstructured interviews.

Interviewer bias is a problem that is difficult to remove. No-one has a blank identity which will have no effect on the responses.

Strengths of structured interviews are:		
It is possible to collate the results into statistics to help see patterns.	The use of an interviewer means that the questions are more likely to be completed. Interviewers are able to encourage people to answer questions and clarify their meanings.	Questions are standardised, which results in answers that are easy to compare. This increases reliability. There is still the chance of high validity levels as people are more likely to be truthful face to face.

Weaknesses of structured interviews are:		
Time consuming and costly as interviewers cost money.	There is a possibility of interviewer bias.	There may still be a problem in getting respondents to cooperate. This will result in a lower response rate. This may affect the representativeness of the sample.

Strengths of unstructured interviews are:		
Answers are in depth and detailed resulting in higher validity.	The interviewer develops a rapport with the respondent. They can evolve questions as the interview develops and ask questions they may never have thought of at the start of the interview. This increases validity.	They result in very rich data which tells us first hand about social life. They are very useful for investigating groups that not much is known about. This again adds to validity.

Weaknesses of unstructured interviews are:		
It is hard to generalise results. The interview may go off topic.	Interviewer bias may result. The personal characteristics of the interviewer is likely to affect the interview as there is a lot of interaction. Whether an interviewer is male or female, white or ethnic minority, young or old is likely to affect the responses.	Unstructured interviews are expensive and time consuming. They are low in reliability because of the uniqueness of each interview.

REVISION BOOSTER

When asked to choose a method and explain why the method would be suitable, it is important to read the question carefully. Make sure that you relate the method to the specific situation described in the question.

Key figure

William Labov noticed in his research on language how interviewer bias happened. He noticed that black people were far more likely to speak openly when interviewed by another black person and in comfortable settings. A white researcher asking them questions in a formal setting gained less valid answers.

Think link

Research methods link closely to theory. For instance, labelling theory is interested in the individual views and meanings of a situation. This makes unstructured interviews or participant observation more useful methods for sociologists who are interested in this.

Effective interviews build trust (rapport) with the participants. This increases the chance of gaining honest answers high in validity.

Knowledge check

1. Describe what is meant by a 'structured interview'.
   (2 marks)
2. Explain two reasons why interviews are useful for sociologists.   (4 marks)
3. Discuss the usefulness of unstructured interviews.
   (12 marks)

Spec spotlight

4.2 Methods of research: different types of observations, the value, practical application and strength of different methods in terms of validity, reliability, ethics, representativeness

Link to textbook

pp 246–247: Different types of sociological observation

AO2 Apply

A sociologist wants to study homeless people. Which type of observation should they use and why? What problems would there be?

Take it further

Sociologists have done some questionable things in their studies. For instance, William H. Whyte illegally voted more than once in an election while studying a street corner group.

Could these activities be justified? Or what about the following?

- Watching people take Class 3 drugs such as heroin?
- Taking part in a fight between rival gangs of football supporters?

Different types of observation

Observation is the most direct type of research used by sociologists. It observes social life first hand.	There are several different types of observation including covert and overt, participant and non-participant. Many studies using observation are qualitative and look for the rich detail of social life through the eyes of the people involved.
Covert observation involves studying people without their knowledge. Their presence as observers of the group is unknown.	Covert observation usually involves participant observation. The observer presents themselves as a member of the group and joins in the activities of the group. There are many good examples of this including James Patrick's *A Glasgow Gang Observed*.
Some observers have an overt role where the group are aware of the presence of the observer.	Being overt has some advantages as the researcher can ask questions, take notes and opt out of anything criminal or anti-social.
It is also possible to be a non-participant observer.	Non-participant observation could involve watching through a glass screen or filming the group. There are some big ethical issues about this, but it does prevent the observer affecting the behaviour of the group studied.

Considerations when using observation

How will the researcher record the data that they are collecting?	The researchers have to decide how to collect their data. If they are a participant observer, they will need to have a good memory and write down notes at the end of each day.
Access to the group being studied may be difficult.	Permission must be sought if studying a group, such as a school or other organisation. The gatekeeper is the person through whom the researcher gains access. In informal groups, such as a gang, the gatekeeper may be a gang member. For example, William H. Whyte gained access to the group through 'Doc' in *Street Corner Society*. The researcher may have to dress or act differently to be accepted.
Ethical issues must be considered.	If joining a criminal or delinquent subculture, what will the researcher do if the group does something illegal? The situation could also become dangerous. Ken Pryce, the British sociologist, disappeared while studying West Indian criminality.
Finding a gatekeeper overcomes the issue of 'getting in' but there may also be a problem of 'getting out'.	Leaving the group may not be easy. Researchers may have made some warm human connections with the group they are studying. This may be difficult for the researcher and in any case raises issues about the ethics of taking advantage of the group studied just to write a piece of research.

What might the weaknesses of snowball sampling be?

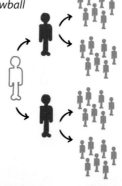
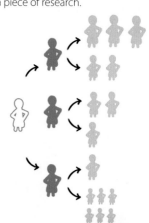

Strengths of covert participant observation are:

First-hand research which sees society close up. High in validity	Avoids the Hawthorne Effect as the people studied are unaware so will not behave differently.	Researcher may discover the answers to questions that they would never have even considered.

Weaknesses of covert participant observation are:

Even though the Hawthorne Effect is avoided, the researcher may still affect the group studied. Their presence may still change things.	Ethical issues. The people being studied do not have the right to informed consent. There is also deception involved if the researcher's identity is concealed.	The researcher may 'go native'. They may become so involved in the group they are observing that they are not unbiased.

Strengths of overt participant observation are:

First-hand research which sees society close up in their normal lives. High in validity.	Trust can be built up allowing the researcher to find out a great deal.	This may be the only way to study some behaviour. Questionnaires and interviews are not likely to be possible to arrange with criminal or deviant groups.

Weaknesses of overt participant observation are:

Relies on the skills of the observer to notice what is happening.	Hawthorne Effect. People being observed may act differently when they know they are being observed.	Low reliability as research is difficult to repeat. The research is very individual and may only be true of one group studied.

A sample should normally represent a fair mix of the population studied.

REVISION BOOSTER

In the exam, follow the question instruction carefully. You have a limited time and cannot waste it. If the question asks you to identify or describe, you do not need to spend time evaluating.

Think link

Studies using participant observation tend to be closely linked with crime and deviance. Gain marks by using studies in more than one answer in your exam. Know three or four studies well, e.g. James Patrick, William H. Whyte, Hannah Gavron etc.

Key figure

William H. Whyte produced one of the most famous and influential studies using participant observation of Italian street corner life. He was able to gain access through a person called 'Doc' and gained a great understanding of the gang. Whyte spent three and a half years living with and becoming part of the group. 'Doc', who was the only member of the group who knew the truth about Whyte, said that his behaviour was changed by Whyte's research. He found himself questioning why he was doing things instead of just acting on instinct.

Knowledge check

1. Describe what is meant by 'overt observation'. **(2 marks)**
2. Explain two reasons why participant observation is used by some sociologists. **(4 marks)**
3. Discuss ethical concerns with the use of observation to study gangs. **(6 marks)**

Spec spotlight

4.2 Methods of research: the value, practical application and strengths and weaknesses of different methods in terms of ethics

4.5 Ethical issues affecting research: informed consent, confidentiality, harm to participants, deception, strategies used by sociologists to address issues.

7.1 The process of research design

Link to textbook

pp 250–251: What are ethics in sociological research?

AO2 Apply

Can you think of ethical considerations for the following research projects?

- *Children who have been bullied at school*
- *Women who have experienced domestic abuse*
- *Studying the lifestyle of homeless people*
- *Gang membership*
- *White-collar crime*

Take it further

Think of two situations when a researcher can justify breaking ethical guidelines?

An example of an ethical issue is the need for informed consent for people taking part in research. Can you think of any examples where there could be exceptions to this in sociology?

Ethics in sociological research

Ethics are based upon the idea of what is right and wrong and standards of behaviour in research carried out by sociologists.	There are strict guidelines for sociological research which are set out by the British Sociological Association. These include guidance on a wide range of issues which are designed to protect the reputation of sociology as an academic discipline. Research which breaks these guidelines harms the possibilities of future research.
Informed consent is one of the most important guidelines for sociologists to follow.	Participants in research have the right to know what they are signing up for. The aims of the research should be clear to participants and the way in which results are going to be reported in public or elsewhere.
Participants have the right to withdraw from research at any time if they are unhappy with the process.	The right of withdrawal is not possible if research is covert. This does not mean that covert research is not possible to do. However, it should only be carried out when there is no other possible method of research. Research like that which James Patrick carried out on Glasgow gangs could not have been carried out openly.
Confidentiality and anonymity are both vital parts of research.	Anonymity requires that the identities of people involved in the research are not revealed. They should not be able to be identified from the information published in the research and are entitled to privacy. Information shared in an interview should be confidential. However, there are situations when a researcher could be in a difficult position. For instance, if a crime is committed or someone is going to be hurt.
Participants should not be put at risk of physical or psychological harm.	It is clear that physical harm is not acceptable as a result of sociological research. However, the studies into gangs and subcultures through participant observation may risk this as the observer may influence events. Psychological harm is more difficult to measure though and could include embarrassment, stress or worry about the process of research. Sociologists should not put themselves in unreasonable danger.
Sociological research should have a worthy purpose.	The findings of sociological research should be used to improve human life in some way. It should not be used to harm or control others.
The reports of sociological findings should not have a negative effect on the people studied.	When James Patrick carried out his study of Glasgow gangs he delayed publishing as he was worried that the publicity might make the situation worse.
Finally, debriefing is a vital part of the process for participants.	Debriefing means that participants are given support to ensure that they do not leave with anxieties about the process that they have taken part in. Skilled counsellors should talk to them and ensure they have not been harmed by the process.

Ethical strengths of Patrick's study are:		
Tim, one of the gang members knew Patrick's real identity. Patrick was honest with this member of the group. He protected all of the group's identity.	Patrick refused to carry a weapon and held back from fights, although this may have placed him in more danger.	Patrick considered ethical issues carefully when deciding to delay reporting his study.

Ethical criticisms of Patrick's study are:		
Patrick was deceiving the gang members every time he met the group.	Patrick was present when the group were behaving anti-socially and breaking the law and may have affected their behaviour.	There was no informed consent. Apart from Tim, none of them knew they were part of a research project.

Support for the argument that sometimes ethics can be ignored is:		
A debrief of the participants after the research can ensure no harm is done.	Sometimes there is no other way of carrying out the research. For instance, criminals and some deviant subcultures will not agree to take part in a questionnaire.	The findings can sometimes be so valuable that it justifies breaching the guidelines.

Support against the argument that sometimes ethics can be ignored is:		
The British Psychological association has drawn up a detailed set of guidance. There is never an excuse to ignore this.	Damage may be done to the reputation of the subject. People may not want to take part in any future research if people have a poor experience of sociological research.	Sociological research can be harmful to individuals. If care is not taken about well-being, then long-term psychological effects could happen.

REVISION BOOSTER

Make links across topics in the syllabus. When you are revising, add these links to your notes and when planning your answers.

Key figure

Paul Willis completed a famous study of boys in a Wolverhampton secondary school in the 1970s. On the one hand his study listened to what the boys had to say and allowed their view of the world to be published and taken seriously. Thousands of people have read about Willis's study and the understanding of social class and educational failure was improved. On the other hand, he saw unpleasant behaviour, such as fighting, racism and homophobia, and allowed this to continue.

Think link

Ethics is useful in answering questions across the whole methods topic. Ethics is particularly useful if you are asked to evaluate a study or method.

Debriefing is an important part of research. This should ensure that participants are not caused any psychological harm or stress through the research process.

Knowledge check

1. Describe what is meant by 'ethics'. **(2 marks)**
2. Identify two ethical issues in the use of unstructured interviews. **(2 marks)**
3. Explain why sociologists should consider ethics when carrying out research. **(4 marks)**

Spec spotlight

4.2 Methods of research: representativeness

4.3 Sampling processes: representative and non-representative sampling techniques

7.1 The process of research design: selection of sampling techniques

Link to textbook

pp 256–257: How do sociologists choose a sampling technique?

AO2 Apply

There are 1000 students in a school. The researcher wants to interview a representative sample of them and has time to interview 100 students.

There are 200 in each year group Y7–11. There are 600 girls and 400 boys. 80 of the students are from ethnic minority groups. 80 of the students have Special Educational Needs.

How many students should be interviewed? How many from each group? Boys? Girls? Year groups? Ethnic minorities? Special Educational Needs students?

How would the researcher choose the sample?

Take it further

As a follow up, the researcher wants to interview students that smoke. How could the researcher get a sample?

Representative sampling techniques

The census taken every ten years in the UK is one piece of research where the aim is to get information about every person.

In most cases there is not time to study the whole population, so a sample is taken. The people that are the aim of the study are called the target population. A sample is drawn from the target population and results are based on this group. For instance, your school could be the target population for a study and a sample of students drawn from this.

In many cases the aim will be to draw a sample that is representative of the target population as a whole.

There are a number of ways of gathering a representative sample. Random samples are gathered using names out of a hat or computer-generated lists. This method is random but not necessarily representative. However, this is a common method used in research.

Systematic samples are also used when a random sample is not easy to generate.

Systematic samples may involve a system such as choosing every tenth name on a list. For instance, choosing every tenth or twentieth name on the school register. Again, this may not be a truly representative sample.

Quota samples are a method of making sure that there is a truly representative sample. Stratified random sampling is another means of achieving this.

A quota sample involves making sure that the sample has the correct proportion of different gender, ethnic or age groups. Stratified random sampling also attempts to ensure that the sample is more representative than using a random sample. The sample would be split into different group types based on class, gender, age, ethnicity etc. and then making sure that the right proportion of that group are selected. For instance, if 8 per cent of the target population are African-Caribbean, then 8 per cent of the sample will be also.

Non-representative sampling techniques

The most common type of sample is an opportunity or convenience sample.

This sort of sample makes no real attempt to be representative and is often used by college students carrying out research. Being non-representative is a disadvantage of this type of sample.

Sometimes non-representative samples may be chosen deliberately.

For instance, John Goldthorpe and David Lockwood wanted to study car workers who were well paid and affluent. Therefore, they deliberately chose people from that group who were not like the general population. A researcher might want to study female doctors from a working-class background and so would choose female doctors from those backgrounds.

The snowball method will also be non-representative.

Snowballing is used for hard-to-reach groups, such as criminal or deviant groups. This involves finding a connection to one member of the group and researching them, while using them as a link to another person and so on. In this way, a sample from the group is gained.

No sampling method is perfect, and each has its limitations.

Both representative and non-representative samples have their uses for sociologists.

Strengths of random sampling are:

Everyone has an equal chance of selection.	It is a fair way of choosing a sample.	Modern technology now makes this easier.

Weaknesses of random sampling are:

The sample may not be representative.	If there are small groups in the target population, they may not be included at all.	Systematic samples are even less likely to be representative.

Strengths of quota sampling are:

It includes the right proportion of different groups.	It is randomly based on the people stopped.	If done correctly it should give a representative sample.

Weaknesses of quota sampling are:

Depends on the honesty of the interviewer who may just want to complete the job and fill their quota so that they get paid. They may not actually interview the right people.	They may only stop people who look as though they are happy to be stopped.	There may be a bias in the sample because of the interviewer.

Strengths of snowball sampling are:

It may be the only sampling method that will work.	Very useful for accessing hard-to-reach groups such as criminals or deviant subcultures, e.g. the homeless, drug addicts.	There is no sampling frame. This is the place where a sample is drawn from, e.g. voters could be drawn from the sampling frame of the electoral register. There is no list of criminals or deviants.

Weaknesses of snowball sampling are:

Not random.	Not representative.	It relies on people volunteering, which may be a particular type of person, which creates bias.

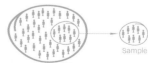

Spec spotlight

4.4 Practical issues affecting research: access to subjects of research, gatekeeper to allow access, time and cost of research

7.1 The process of research design: choosing a research area, choosing a method

Link to textbook

pp 252–253: How do sociologists make choices about research?

AO2 Apply

What practical considerations would affect research into the following areas?

- *Heroin addicts*
- *Graffiti artists*
- *Radicalisation*
- *Survivors of domestic abuse*
- *Football hooliganism*

Take it further

The government is offering to fund research into the effect of changes to the benefits system in the UK. There has been a lot of criticism of the new system in the media. You are a committed sociologist who seeks the truth about society. What concerns would you have in agreeing to take on this research project?

Most research will require access to people. There is often a gatekeeper who the researcher needs to gain access from. Can you think of any examples of gatekeepers for different places you might wish to research?

Practical issues and choosing what to study

One of the most important issues is in choosing an area of social life that a sociologist wants to study. Personal interest is likely to shape this decision.	Sociologists are likely to choose something which they feel strongly about or are particularly interested in. However, it may not always be possible to study what they want to because of the need for funding. This is essential and may be from universities, business, charities or the government. These groups control the money and will affect which subjects are chosen for research.
Research that has already been done will have a big impact on the choice of research.	If there is a lot of previous research or other information available this may influence the researcher. For instance, if there are a lot of official statistics on crime available, a researcher may decide to study this.
The trends of the times are likely to affect the choice of research.	The media may be featuring lots of stories about a particular issue in society. Social media, fake news and cybercrime may be likely to attract funding for this reason and so may be chosen by sociologists.
The subject the researcher wishes to study may be easy to access.	A researcher may have a contact which allows access to the group they wish to study. For instance, in *A Glasgow Gang Observed*, through his job as a youth worker, James Patrick met Tim, the gang member. This encouraged his choice of research area. Some areas may be difficult to gain access to, which may put researchers off.

Practical issues affecting choice of research method

Once an area has been chosen, the researcher has to begin planning the research.	One of the most important choices is in the type of research methods to use. Some researchers may believe strongly in one approach over others. For instance, Ann Oakley, a feminist , believed that unstructured interviews are a more female-friendly style of research. She criticised traditional structured interviews for having a typical male-dominated relationship style.
Some methods may not be practically possible.	If a researcher wishes to study bullying in schools, then clearly participant observation is not going to be possible for ethical reasons. More sensitive methods, such as unstructured interviews, will be needed to gain information about difficult topics. Researchers should also not put themselves in danger.
The personal characteristics of the researcher may influence the method chosen.	If a researcher is female and wished to study a sensitive area for women, such as domestic violence, then this may be appropriate. A male wishing to research the same area might need to think carefully about how they would go about this. Similarly, a white researcher might find it difficult to investigate racism towards ethnic minorities.
Time available may influence the style of research.	Longitudinal studies which follow groups of people over a long period of time require a lot of money and a long-term commitment in terms of time and resources. Resources include computers, interviewers' wages, printing and postage.

Strengths of the idea that sociologists are able to freely decide on their research are:		
Sociologists have personal interests and their own experiences, which influence their research choices.	Sociologists often favour certain styles of research. However, many prefer to use mixed methods depending on what they are studying.	Sociologists are often strongly influenced by one of the main theories. For instance, Marxists and feminists are likely to pursue their beliefs strongly when deciding upon research. New Right sociologists are concerned about changes in society and will pursue research that questions this.

Weaknesses of the idea that sociologists are able to freely decide on their research are:		
Time is a strong limitation on research. There may be pressure to publish reports which may mean research is rushed and less thorough.	Funding is also a huge influence on both the choice of topic and, more worryingly, the findings. A group who have paid for research will expect findings which help persuade people of their views. A sociologist who comes up with the 'wrong' results for a company may not get any further work.	Access to a group of people is likely to be a big influence on the choice of research and the method chosen. Personal characteristics of the researcher are also likely to affect research. This includes age, gender, class and ethnicity.

Strengths of Venkatesh's study are:		
Venkatesh managed to gain access to a gang called the 'Black Kings' in Chicago between about 1989 and 1996. He was given access through a gatekeeper called JT and was able to observe them first hand over a long period of time.	His book Gang Leader for a Day was published relatively recently in 2009 so is more up to date.	Venkatesh's personal characteristics of being a South Asian male allowed him to access a group that was African-American. This would not have been possible if he were white.

Weaknesses of Venkatesh's study are:		
JT was only a low-level member of the gang. The higher levels of the organisation were very hard for Venkatesh to discover.	Venkatesh wrote a field diary of his conversations and observations but this relied on his memory.	Venkatesh became so involved with the group he often acted like one of them.

Funding may be a huge practical problem for research. The government, businesses or charities may choose to sponsor research. Could the sponsor affect the results of research? How?

Key figure

Sudhir Venkatesh conducted a study of gang life in Chicago. The gang were a crack-dealing gang who he studied for about 18 months over a period of seven years. Venkatesh used participant observation and was able to see some of the activities first hand. This involved lots of criminal activity including drugs and violence. One interesting fact is that he began by attempting to do a questionnaire with people who lived in the 'Projects'. He was surrounded quickly by gang members who were part of the Black Kings. He realised that asking questions was pointless and that to understand them he needed to live with them and see life through their eyes. He put himself in considerable danger but took the practical opportunity to gain access.

Think link

Practical issues may be used to help evaluate arguments about different topics. For instance, practical issues may influence why there is less research into corporate crime or white-collar crime. Think about the practical reasons why this may not happen.

Knowledge check

1. Describe what is meant by the term 'gatekeeper'. **(2 marks)**
2. Identify two practical issues affecting research. **(2 marks)**
3. Explain two ways in which practical issues may influence the research of sociologists.
   (4 marks)

Link to textbook

pp 254–255: Establishing an aim and/or hypothesis

pp 258–259: How do sociologists plan successful research?

Spec spotlight

4.4 Practical issues affecting research: access to subjects of research, gatekeeper to allow access, time and cost of research

7.1 The process of research design: choosing a research area, establishing an aim and/or hypothesis, choosing a method, use of pilot study, selection of sampling techniques, analysis of data

AO2 Apply

Decide how you would carry out a piece of research into people's views on voting in the EU referendum.

- *What research question hypothesis could you develop?*
- *What sampling method would you use?*
- *Where would you get your sample from?*
- *What research method would you use?*

Take it further

Carry out a short pilot study using five questions. What changes would you make to your questions?

Research design

There are several stages involved in the planning of successful research.	Choosing a topic area, assessing cost, time, funding and availability of people and information are all parts of planning successful research. Trying to ensure a sociologist's own views and beliefs do not impact the research is also key.
Once the topic is decided upon, decisions should be made about the sample type and research questions must be designed.	Research questions may be broad, but some sociologists prefer to develop a scientific hypothesis. A hypothesis is a statement which the sociologist tests out through the collection of research data. For instance, a hypothesis may be: 'Criminal subcultures are the most important cause of crime in the UK'. Data would be collected to find out how far this statement is true.
Key terms in the study must be explained clearly so that anyone reading the research knows what they mean.	Any key term like 'criminal subculture' must be defined. For instance, a criminal subculture could be defined as a group with its own norms and values that involve deliberate law-breaking behaviour. It may also be useful to turn the key term into something that can be measured. This is called 'operationalising the concept'. For example, a criminal subculture could be broken down into different parts, such as violent behaviour, theft, fraud, illegal drugs etc. This makes it easier to measure.
The style of research must be decided.	The research method or methods must be chosen. Lots of factors may influence this choice including the availability of a sample, ethics, gatekeeper or permission to go to a place to study. The researcher may have a preferred method.
Once the hypothesis/research question and a method are decided upon, timescales and costings need to be carefully considered.	The best thing for a researcher to do at this stage is to carry out a pilot study. For anyone starting out in research this may seem like an unnecessary stage, but it can result in much less work in the long run.
A pilot study can help avoid expensive mistakes in research.	A trial run of the questionnaire or interview can reveal problems that may not be obvious to the researcher. This includes the misunderstanding of questions by the respondents. The pilot study can quickly reveal these unforeseen problems and enable the questions to be rewritten using simpler or different language. Sometimes extra questions are needed to tease out the information required.
There are many good reasons for choosing to carry out a pilot study.	A pilot study may highlight problems with cooperation, validity or the time taken to complete interviews. A pilot study may be needed to secure the funding for the research.
Once the full study has been carried out, decisions have to be made about how to analyse the data.	There may be a lot of data and it will need to be analysed so that patterns can be seen. Decisions can be made about how to present the data to others. Qualitative data often has a lot of detail. Sometimes researchers will look through the data for patterns and simplify it.

REVISION BOOSTER

Prepare for questions that ask you to consider a suitable research method in a certain situation. Think through your reasons for choosing different methods.

Many sociologists have tried to apply the same processes as scientists to find out about society. Creating a hypothesis and testing it out are a part of this process.

Think link
Draw together all the different parts of the research methods topic. It is important to link up all the influences on research and key things to evaluate.

Strengths of the idea that practical issues affect planning research the most are:

The availability of a sample may encourage research on a certain subject.	A link to a gatekeeper is an important practical issue that can make or break research.

Weaknesses of the idea that practical issues affect planning research the most are:

Sociologists have very strong beliefs and may find a way to study something they are most interested in.	The information already available may have a great effect on the choice of study.	The theoretical background of the researcher will be a big influence on research choices. A Marxist or feminist will have clear ideas about what they wish to study.

Key figure

The **ESRC Economic and Social Research Council** are one of the main sources for funding of research. They publish very clear guidance about how to plan research. This includes the offer of training and support and how to measure success. Most ESRC funding comes from the government, which may affect what research is agreed.

Sociological research requires a great deal of planning. Lots of money may be involved in research and it is important to spend it wisely. Sociological research is not easy and there are many things to consider.

Knowledge check

1. Describe what is meant by 'hypothesis'. **(2 marks)**
2. Explain why a sociologist might choose to study poverty. **(4 marks)**
3. Discuss what sociologists would need to consider when planning a piece of research into shoplifting. **(6 marks)**

Spec spotlight

4.2 Methods of research: quantitative and qualitative methods, the value, practical application and strength of different methods in terms of validity, reliability, ethics, representativeness, mixed methods approaches

7.1 The process of research design: usefulness of mixed methods approach

Link to textbook

pp 260–261: Why do sociologists sometimes use mixed methods?

AO2 Apply

A sociologist has decided to use questionnaires in a research project on the norms and values of different cultures living in the UK. The pilot study has shown that the questions are not producing very useful information. It seems that the questions are not finding out enough information about the cultures. What advice would you have for the sociologist? What else could they do?

Take it further

Explain why mixed methods would help this study. Use sociological language to justify your answer.

Two approaches to sociology

There have traditionally been two approaches to sociological methods.	One view has been that sociology should be about collecting lots of data in the form of quantitative data. This approach looks for patterns and tries to come up with the laws of society. Questionnaires and official statistics are popular with this approach.
The second approach is about investigating the meanings that people have.	This second approach looks for qualitative data in the form of detailed descriptions of society. Participant observation and unstructured interviews are the classic research methods used by the sociologists who preferred this approach.
There was a big debate between approaches about whether sociology could or should try to gather information in the same way as science.	In fact, most sociologists have realised that there are many practical advantages in using more than one method in their research. Many famous studies use more than one method. This approach is known as the mixed methods approach.
Mixed methods have been adopted by sociologists for practical reasons.	Since the 1970s, the mixed methods approach has become the most popular. Paul Feyerabend, an Austrian philosopher, was one of the biggest influences on this idea. He said that there should be no rules about research and that sociologists should use whatever methods work best.

Reasons why the mixed methods approach is used:

To check that the data collected is accurate.	This can help a piece of research to have both validity and reliability. The use of questionnaires mixed with unstructured interviews can give a researcher the best of both worlds. They are able to use standardised questions gaining reliability, yet also use unstructured interviews to gain the actual world view of those studied.
Sometimes it may be useful to use methods in a sequence.	Observation or unstructured interviews may be a good idea as a first step for a researcher. This is especially true if they are studying a group or place that they do not know much about. Using a qualitative method first may help them decide on the questions that they need to ask in their quantitative questionnaire.
Mixed methods is also useful to cross-check research.	Using a different method is a simple way of checking to see if it finds the same thing.
Other forms of cross-checking in research exist which are called triangulation.	This can include checking the work of one researcher against the work of another or trying the research out in a different place.

When sociologists mix methods, one method may dominate the others. For example, the statistics may create headlines and the qualitative detail may be missed.

Strengths of mixed methods approach are:

A broader picture can be gathered of the part of society being studied.

Two or more methods can complement each other gaining reliability and validity.

More data means a greater understanding is gathered.

Weaknesses of mixed methods approach are:

The researcher needs to be highly skilled at using different methods.

The cost of employing different methods can be great. It can also be very time consuming.

Analysing the results is very difficult. Sometimes one method may dominate the report. Often this is the method which collected quantitative data.

Weaknesses of concentrating on one method for research are:

Using a single method can only provide either quantitative or qualitative data, two or more methods can provide both types of data.

Findings are not cross checked. Two or more methods can help this to be sure of research finding.

Two methods can provide a fuller picture, with both reliability and validity. Eileen Barker used the unstructured interviews to help create hypotheses for her participant observation.

Disadvantages of using mixed methods are:

Using several methods can be time-consuming and therefore costly.

Sometimes the data from one method, for instance the statistics, can dominate the research.

SOCIAL RESEARCH METHODS

OBSERVATION

CONTENT ANALYSIS

SURVEY

INTERVIEW

FOCUS GROUP

ETHNOGRAPHY

FAMILY HISTORY

HISTORICAL METHOD

CASE STUDY

There is a wide range of methods to choose from for sociologists. Usually when mixing methods there will be a mix of quantitative and qualitative.

Key figure

Eileen Barker's *The Making of a Moonie* is one of the classic studies which used mixed methods. Her study of the religious group the Moonies involved six years of participant observation, unstructured interviews and questionnaires given to a large sample to produce the large amount of data on which she based her book.

Think link

Bring mixed methods into other questions about research methods. If asked to discuss questionnaire or participant observation, remember that they may be used as part of a mixed methods approach.

Knowledge check

1. Describe what is meant by a 'mixed methods approach'. **(2 marks)**

2. Explain two reasons why a mixed methods approach is useful for sociologists. **(4 marks)**

3. 'Sociologists will be successful using one method for effective research.' Do you agree with this view? **(6 marks)**

Spec spotlight

4.1 Usefulness of different types of data: primary and secondary data, quantitative and qualitative data, sources of secondary data, usefulness of these types of data to sociologists

4.2 Methods of research: the value, practical application and strength of different methods in terms of validity, reliability, ethics, representativeness

Link to textbook

pp 262–263: How useful is sociological research?

AO2 Apply

A study has been investigating the influence of hip hop music on British teenagers. The researcher is a 56-year-old white British man from Cornwall. He has decided to devise a questionnaire with closed questions about rap music.

What advice would you give him about this research? What strengths and weaknesses might the research have?

Take it further

Is it possible to devise a study that is high in reliability and validity? How could you do this?

Reliability in sociology is about whether a different researcher who repeated the study could expect to get roughly the same results. If this could not be expected, the study is low in reliability.

Evaluating sociological research

There are a number of things to consider when you evaluate a sociological study.	Some of these you would use to review any piece of evidence whether it was sociological or not. For instance, is the research up to date and who collected the data? If data was collected by someone, what was their purpose? The data may be biased in some respect.
Sociology has four main things to consider when evaluating research. The acronym REVS may help you remember: Reliability, Ethics, Validity and Sample.	Reliability assesses whether the research is repeatable. The sociologist should provide clear details of how they collected the data and the questions used. To be high in reliability someone else should be able to repeat the study with the expectation of roughly similar results. If the study was repeated in another place or time, the results could then be compared.
Ethics have been covered in some detail on an earlier page. Studies are open to criticism if they have not followed ethical guidelines without good justification.	Validity is about the extent to which the research data shows a true picture of society. A number of things may cause validity to be low. These include a lack of honesty from respondents who may be dishonest for a variety of reasons. These include embarrassment, social desirability and interviewer bias. Validity may be low if questions are asked which do not allow respondents to put forward their full opinions.
The nature of the sample is open to be criticised. The sample should aim to represent the population studied.	In many cases, sociologists aim for a representative sample of the target population. A representative sample should include a fair representation of class, gender, ethnicity, age and any other significant factors. Non-representative samples are acceptable if the aim is to target a particular subgroup, such as criminals.

Evaluating different research methods and types of data

Every research method and source of data in sociology is open to criticism, yet they also all have strengths and give different advantages.	Quantitative data will always have the benefit of being able to observe patterns and generate ideas about society. Studies which collect quantitative data should be able to ensure that it is high in reliability, providing methods used are made clear. However, the data collected may lack validity. For instance, the use of closed questions may have trapped respondents into a limited range of answers.
Qualitative data has the advantage of more detail and description.	Qualitative data may often have been gathered in a way that lacks reliability. The methods used to collect qualitative data are often quite individual and are not easy for a different researcher to imitate. Methods used by James Patrick and R.E. Dobash and R. Dobash require a very particular study which is hard to copy. However, qualitative data often has a great deal of validity.
Questionnaires and structured interviews often have high levels of reliability.	The use of standardised questions means that there is a great deal of reliability. Official statistics may also have the advantage of reliability. However, these methods tend to have lower rates of validity.
Participant observation and unstructured interviews tend to have high levels of validity.	These styles of research tend to gather detailed information that offers high levels of validity. The individual way in which these methods gather information means that reliability is low. Validity and reliability may be seen a little like a seesaw. When a method gains high validity it often loses out in reliability and vice versa. This has led many sociologists to use mixed methods to gain the best of both worlds.

Strengths of Jackson's study of schools are:

She had researched the background of schools and tried to select a mix of schools to be representative.

There was a mixture of methods which added reliability and validity.

The interview data is very rich in detail and produces a real picture of the world of students.

Weaknesses of Jackson's study of schools are:

The schools were all in the north of England.

Samples are from one age group only, although this year group is in the middle of secondary school.

From 2006 so the study is already beginning to date.

Strengths of Willis's *Learning to Labour* are:

Paul Willis studied the boys for 18 months. This is a long time. Ethically the study gave the boys a voice they may not get very often.

The school selected was all white, but Willis selected it because it represented the types of school attended by working-class students.

Wide range of methods used by Willis including interviews, group discussions and participant observation. This increased validity.

Weaknesses of Willis's *Learning to Labour* are:

Ethically Willis saw the boys behaving in an anti-social way – fighting, racism, vandalism – but allowed this to happen.

Sample size was very low with only 12 boys.

Reliability is low as the research is difficult to repeat exactly as Willis did.

Has the research study gained a true picture of reality? If so then the study is said to be high in validity.

Key figure

Carolyn Jackson investigated the fear of failure amongst secondary school students in 2006. She discovered that their reactions to the fear of failure were often defensive. Her study included questionnaire data from 800 students and interviews with 153 students (13- to 14-year-olds) and 30 teachers. The interviews were unstructured and were high in validity. The respondents were from six secondary schools in the north of England. Four of the schools were mixed, one all boys and one all girls. She used data from Ofsted and the schools themselves to try and make sure there was a range of schools included.

REVISION BOOSTER

Remember the REVS acronym if you are asked to evaluate a method or study: Reliability, Ethics, Validity and Sample. There ought to be a comment that you can make using these.

Think link

Methods links to every topic. Whenever you are asked to evaluate, remember to include criticisms of research methods if possible. This could gain valuable marks.

Knowledge check

1. Describe what is meant by 'reliability'. **(2 marks)**

2. Describe what is meant by 'validity'. **(2 marks)**

3. Explain two reasons why questionnaires may lack validity. **(4 marks)**

Preparing for the exam

WJEC Eduqas GCSE Sociology includes two papers. Both papers last for 1 hour 45 minutes, which adds up to 105 minutes each. Each paper is worth 50 per cent of the total mark.

Paper 1 Understanding Social Processes

Six questions

- Question 1: Mix and match from across the paper (4 marks)
- Questions 2 and 3: Key concepts and processes of cultural transmission
- Question 4: Family
- Question 5: Education
- Question 6: Sociological research methods

Paper 2 Understanding Social Structures

Seven questions

- Question 1: Mix and match from across the paper (4 marks)
- Questions 2, 3, 4 and 5: Social differentiation and stratification

Important note: Question 2 requires students to show skill AO1 demonstrating their understanding of sociological evidence presented in different written, visual and numerical forms. Students are expected to be able to show that they can observe key patterns and trends in data.

- Question 6: Crime and deviance
- Question 7: Applied methods of sociological enquiry

The main topic areas (Family, Education and Crime) are worth 29–30 marks each on the Sample Assessment Materials.

On Paper 1 Key concepts and processes of cultural transmission is worth 19 marks.

On Paper 2 Social differentiation and differentiation is worth 55 marks on the SAMs.

Questions on research methods form 18 marks on Paper 1 and 11 marks on Paper 2.

AO stands for Assessment Objective. Over the whole exam:

- 40% of the marks are for AO1 – **Demonstrate** knowledge and understanding of sociological theories, concepts, evidence and methods.
- 40% of the marks are for AO2 – **Apply** knowledge and understanding of sociological theories, concepts, evidence and methods.
- 20% of the marks are for AO3 – **Analyse and evaluate** sociological theories, concepts, evidence and methods in order to construct arguments, make judgements and draw conclusions.

Type of exam questions

The type of exam questions and amount of marks awarded relate closely to the skills required in the answers. There may be some variation in the format of the papers, but both papers will assess the three skills AO1, AO2 and AO3. Questions may assess one of these skills or a combination of them. The mark schemes make this clear.

AO Keywords	Example question	
AO1: Describe, identify, outline, define, explain	Identify a value in the passage above.	**(1 mark)**
	Describe what is meant by 'identity'.	**(2 marks)**
	Outline how family structures have changed in contemporary UK.	**(4 marks)**
	Define the term 'bourgeoisie'.	**(2 marks)**
	Explain how the media creates moral panics.	**(5 marks)**
AO2: Explain, identify	Explain reasons for differential educational achievement of some ethnic minority groups.	**(4 marks)**
	Identify a research method that would be suitable to study people's online shopping habits.	**(1 mark)**
AO1 + AO2: Identify and explain, explain, explain using examples	Identify and explain reasons for changes in patterns of marriage in the UK.	**(4 marks)**
	Explain the difference between absolute and relative poverty.	**(4 marks)**
	Explain, using examples, the effects of labelling in schools.	**(4 marks)**
	Explain why child-rearing patterns have changed in the UK.	**(8 marks)**
AO2 + AO3: Explain and evaluate	Explain and evaluate the strengths of using questionnaires for research into school attendance.	**(6 marks)**
AO1, AO2 + AO3: Do you agree with this view? Discuss, assess	'Crime is caused by poverty.' Do you agree with this view?	**(15 marks)**
	Discuss the usefulness of participant observation in research.	**(12 marks)**
	Discuss the problem of social exclusion.	**(9 marks)**

Notice that AO3 questions are always assessed along with other skills. AO3 questions for the sections on Family, Education and Crime and deviance are worth 15 marks. Those for the section on Social differentiation and stratification are worth 9 marks. The section on Research Methods has AO3 questions worth 6 and 12 marks.

What to do for a Grade 9

Top Class AO1: includes detailed relevant knowledge and uses sociological language throughout.

- Stronger answer: 'Willis's study took place in Wolverhampton and showed how the subculture of a group of working-class boys led to them underachieving in education.'
- Weaker answer: 'One study found that a group of boys messed about in school and failed. There was another group who were cleverer.'

There doesn't necessarily have to be a huge amount of writing, but what you write should be precise. Name the sociologist, when and where the study was done, and include the main concepts and points made.

Top class AO2: uses the stem of the question in the answer.

- Stronger answer: 'Hargreaves study shows that teachers labelled boys in the top stream as successes. They were successful at school. This shows that labelling can affect educational success.'
- Weaker answer: 'The boys in Hargreaves study were successful when they were labelled successful.' Relevant but no link to the question.

Top class AO3: shows analysis and judgement commenting on the importance of different factors. The most basic level of answer simply states your point: 'One criticism is that the study is really old.' An intermediate level will involve adding context to the answer.

- Stronger answer: 'Willis's study supports the idea that cultural factors are more important than material factors, yet is out of date. Working-class boys in the 21st century may be very different and material factors may be more important now.'

- Weaker answer: 'Willis's study was done a long time ago and may not be useful.' This example is not set in the context of the question.

An expert level answer will add further explanation to make the point thorough and will finish with 'This shows that…' or 'Therefore…' for example.

- 'Willis's study supports the idea that cultural factors are more important than material factors, yet is out of date. Working-class boys in the 21st century may be very different and material factors may be more important now. Working-class families may not be able to buy computers and Internet access, which help educational success in the 21st century. Therefore, material factors may be more important than when Willis did his study.'

In the AO3 Evaluation sections of this book, many strengths and weaknesses of the various theories, concepts, sociological ideas are given, but you will need to apply them to analyse and evaluate the specific exam question on the day. The more strengths and criticisms you know, the more options are available.

▶ Context is king

Questions that offer marks for evaluation also require application. The two skills working together give you the best chance of securing a high grade. Good evaluation points are always applied to the question.

▶ Top class extended writing

Make sure that you organise your ideas clearly. Writing a new paragraph for each main idea is a certain way to achieve this.

Improve your style by linking the next paragraph in with an opening statement: 'Contrastingly, Marxists emphasise the importance of social class rather than gender as a cause of crime.'

Avoid the list approach. If you simply list facts you are just scoring for knowledge and understanding. It is how you apply the studies, rather than the number of studies or concepts you know, that examiners are looking for. The extended writing questions are looking for more than just knowledge. They want to see you apply, analyse and evaluate.

▶ Timings

There are 100 marks on each paper. The two papers last 105 minutes each, which averages around one mark per minute. However, you would be well advised to allow time to plan for the longer questions to allow thinking and planning time. This could be done by spending less time on shorter one- and two-mark questions, which should not require lots of writing.

Writing a lot does not necessarily mean a high score. You can repeat yourself and wander away from the main points. Examiners will realise this and are not easily fooled by the length of an answer. They are looking for clear responses that tackle the questions in a direct fashion.

Top Tips

Describe and outline: Questions with this in the title are usually looking for description and are a chance for you to show knowledge and understanding. Examples can help to show your understanding.

Define: These questions are looking for a definition and again an example may help to do this.

Identify: These questions are usually looking for short answers which get to the point of identifying something. If they also feature the word 'explain' then they are likely to require more description.

You will sometimes need to show that you can apply your knowledge, for example in a question which asks you to identify a research method.

Explain: Often requires reasons, especially if followed by the word 'reasons'! Or 'Why?' Sometimes it may require a difference to be explained. If it asks for examples, make sure you give more than one in your answer.

Discuss: These questions are always looking for the debate and more than one view of an issue or question.

Assess: Often looking for an evaluation of a view or theory. Examiners will expect to see different views as well as strengths and weaknesses.

Do you agree? These questions are looking for analysis and evaluation. Even though it asks whether you agree, stronger answers will avoid saying 'I think' and use neutral language. 'The evidence would suggest that…' or 'The arguments seem to suggest that…'.

▶ How much to write?

- 1–2 marks usually require short answers, and some may not require full sentences.
- 4 marks often means looking for two main ideas at least and would probably need around 100 words divided into paragraphs.
- 5 marks usually means extended knowledge questions looking for around 125 words.

Therefore, 25 words per mark is a reasonable guideline. Writing styles vary and some students can write very concise arguments that gain marks quickly.

Extended writing is what it says and requires a real effort to write an answer of reasonable length. However, attempting all the questions is very important in the exam.

Effective revision

There are many different styles of revision and it is important to find the one that is most effective for you. However, whichever strategy you choose, make sure that it is an active form of revision. Simply sitting reading your notes is unlikely to be effective and can be very boring! Glancing through your notes regularly may help, but you need to spend time on focused activities which could involve you rewriting your notes or summarising content as a diagram for example.

▶ Memory

A simple way of looking at memory is that it is divided into two. The first part of memory involves a working or short-term memory. This part of the memory can only hold a small amount of facts for a short time. Try remembering two mobile phone numbers at once – it is not very easy and can make you feel very flustered.

Revision can make you feel like this and you may worry about the amount of content you have to remember. Luckily, we have another part of our memory which is designed to help.

The secret is to store the information in the other part of your memory, which is your long-term memory. Long-term memory has a huge capacity but we need to be good at retrieving the information. The way to do this is by repetition and using the information regularly. Most people can remember their own mobile number because they are used to giving it out regularly. The only other ones they remember are the ones they use often, such as those of parents, boyfriend or girlfriend!

You need to find ways of using the information in an active way that you will remember. You also need to be systematic and break the work up into manageable sections.

▶ **Ideas for revision**

- There are six main topics for this exam. For each one, make a list of the main topic areas and key words that are on the syllabus.
- Make notes of your class notes. Make notes of the notes of your notes until you have a whole topic on one piece of paper. You can always go back to the more detailed notes if you need to.
- Create revision cards for all of the key words and studies. On the back of the cards include more detail and linked ideas. e.g. 'Key word: **Material factors**'. This is likely to be used in the topic of education.' On the back of the cards include a definition and other linked ideas.

Front of card

Back of card

MATERIAL FACTORS

Use with education topic.

Definition – Material factors refers to money and what money can buy

Healthy diet   Books   Computers   Internet access
Study or quiet room   Poverty   Educational trips
Private schooling   Private tutors

Halsey study shows material factors important.
Other factors to compare to – Cultural factors,
School factors

- Devise posters for yourself with key words and studies.
- Draw mind maps and spider diagrams for a useful visual snapshot of themes and ideas.
- Look at exam-style questions. Use the examples in this book and use the stem words featured in this section to create your own questions. Practise planning answers and writing paragraphs for the answers. At first, use your notes to help you and gradually withdraw the use of your notes so that you are ready for the exam. This is ultimately going to be the best preparation that you can do. After all, you would not prepare for a marathon without doing any running.
- Practise writing introductions under timed conditions. This is a good way of organising ideas.

▶ How long should I revise for?

When you have a session of revision you need to have fairly regular breaks. Most schools have lessons of 50 or 60 minutes. After this, most people need to have a break. This is important as it allows your brain the chance to process the information. Therefore, revise for 40–50 minutes and then take a break for 10 minutes. Then do another 40–50 minutes and break again. You also need to get plenty of sleep to allow your long-term memory to process the information.

Above all, you need to find what works for you.

Understanding how the mark scheme works

At the time of writing, there have been no previous exams, so there are no grade boundaries. In fact, grade boundaries will vary from year to year for each individual paper. However, you can get a sense of what the mark scheme is looking for by looking closely at the marks available.

▶ AO1 questions

Describe what is meant by 'culture'. **(2 marks)**

The mark scheme allows 2 marks for AO1 – Knowledge and understanding.

Weaker answer

Culture is a way of life for people.

Stronger answer

Culture is a shared, learned way of life which includes norms, values, beliefs, dress, clothes and music. For example, the Inuit have a culture based around hunting and living in a harsh environment.

> The second answer is obviously much stronger as it features a clearer, more detailed definition. It also shows a greater knowledge of what culture is and knowledge of examples.

Outline how family structures have changed in the UK today. **(4 marks)**

The mark scheme allows 4 marks for AO1 – Knowledge and understanding.

Weaker answer

Family structures have changed in the UK today because children are the centre of family life now. There is also more divorce and people not having as many children.

Stronger answer

Family structures have changed in the UK today in many ways. One main way is that the size of families has become smaller. Contraception has meant that families choose to have fewer children. Women also prefer to have fewer children because more women have careers now.

A second way is that the roles of husband and wife have changed. Traditional gender roles of breadwinner and domestic housewife have been replaced by joint roles. New man has appeared and helps with the housework. Men are also more involved in child care. Women also go to work more often,

Both answers mention two ways, but the second one includes more detail on each way. It also shows a greater knowledge and understanding linking together different idea about changes in the family structure. The second one could have been strengthened further with examples.

▶ **AO2 questions**

Explain reasons for differential educational achievement of some ethnic minority groups. **(4 marks)**

The mark scheme allows 4 marks for AO2 – Application questions require knowledge and understanding but also require the student to use the information skilfully to answer the question set.

Weaker answer

Some ethnic minority groups achieve more than others. Chinese children achieve statistically more than white children. Bangladeshi children have been achieving more because they work hard.

Stronger answer

Educational achievement varies between different ethnic groups. There are a number of different reasons for this. One of the most common reasons is material factors. Ethnic minority groups are more likely to live in poverty and so will be affected by this. Poverty means that they may not be able to afford those things which help educational success, such as trips out, computers, Internet access or even a good place to do homework. White working-class children are affected by this, especially boys.

A second reason would be factors in school such as racism and labelling. Evidence suggests that black children are more likely to be excluded from school. The Stephen Lawrence case suggested that racism is found in many places in the UK, possibly including schools. The curriculum may also be biased towards white people and may not help ethnic minority groups achieve educational success.

The first answer does not really apply the knowledge to the question title. This is going to make it difficult for the examiner to award any marks. The reason suggested is very basic. The student had knowledge of differences in ethnic groups' educational attainment but was not able to apply it.

The second answer features at least two explanations: material and school factors, but also begins to hint at cultural factors. It is much stronger and applies a greater range of knowledge showing an understanding. Cultural factors could have been expanded further and studies added including those on anti-school subcultures.

Exam practice and techniques

▶ AO2 + AO3 question

> Explain and evaluate the strengths of using questionnaires for research into school attendance.   **(6 marks)**

The mark scheme allows 3 marks for AO2 Application and 3 marks for AO3 Evaluation.

Weaker answer

Questionnaires are good for finding out about school attendance. You could give the children them to fill out in tutor time. They would be really quick and you could get a lot back and find out tons of information. One strength is that they wouldn't take long to fill out. You could draw graphs of the answers.

Stronger answer

Questionnaires are a suitable method for finding about school attendance. The answers could be collected quickly from a large sample of parents, students and teachers. The large sample would help to make the research representative which means that you could cover people from the full range of the population including different ethnic and gender groups.

Questionnaires are also easy to repeat because they have standard questions. This means that they can be repeated in different places with high reliability. Statistics can be compared.

However, you should also be careful when using questionnaires to study school attendance because some children and parents may lie about school attendance because they do not want to admit they are missing school. This makes questionnaires low in validity as they do not show a true picture. Validity could also be low if the questions are not carefully designed. Respondents may not be able to give the answer that they really want to. The answers also lack detail.

> The first answer lacks use of specialist terminology but does apply relevant knowledge and understanding to explain the strengths of questionnaires and how they could be applied to research school attendance. It is repetitive and lacks development. Evaluation is lacking because it does not show any weaknesses to balance it out.
>
> The second answer features application of knowledge and understanding and explains accurately in detail the strengths of questionnaires for research into school attendance. The question does not ask specifically for weaknesses, but these inevitably help to give the answer its evaluative edge. This is a strong answer but still lacks a concluding sentence to link to the specifics of the question. This could improve it further still.

▶ AO1+AO2 question

> Explain reasons why official criminal statistics should be treated carefully by sociologists.   **(8 marks)**

The mark scheme allows 4 marks for AO1 Knowledge and Understanding and also 4 marks for AO2 Application, requiring the student to use the information skilfully to answer the question set.

Weaker answer

Crime statistics are not always true. The problem is that the people do not always report them to the police. They might be scared or think it is only a little thing and not worth bothering the police with. Some crimes no one even knows about or no one is really bothered about like litter. The police also don't bother recording everything as they want to make it look like they are good at keeping crime from happening. The ones that sociologists don't know about are called the hidden figure of crime.

> The answer receives marks out of four for each skill. The first answer has two reasons contained within which are non-reported and non-recorded crime and shows partial knowledge of official statistics of crime. However, there is very little evidence of sociological language and concepts, with the exception of the hidden figure of crime. There is some application to answer the question although this is limited.

Stronger answer

There are many reasons why official statistics should be treated carefully by sociologists. Firstly, official statistics on crime are produced by the government and rely on police statistics and victim studies. The Crime Survey for England and Wales is published every year. One of the problems is that not all crime is reported or recorded. There are a multitude of reasons for crime being unrecorded or unreported. These include victims thinking the crime is too small, being afraid or embarrassed to report it or perhaps they know the criminal. For instance, victims of sexual harassment may be embarrassed or afraid to report it. A campaign like the #MeToo campaign may affect figures as more people come forward.

The true crime figure can never be known and the unknown figure is referred to as the 'hidden' or 'dark' figure of crime. The police often change the way they record crime and are under pressure to keep figures down affecting the accuracy of the statistics.

There are other sociological factors which affect the statistics. For instance, the police make decisions about how to police different areas. These may be based on stereotypes and racist ideas. Black people are six times more likely to be stopped and searched than white people. This affects the crime figures. Marxists, such as Frank Pearce, claim that the crimes of the ruling class are ignored, and more arrests made for working-class or blue-collar crime. Moral panics also affect the rate of arrests as they encourage the police to focus more closely on certain crimes. This may cause deviancy amplification and increase the crime rate.

The second answer features a good deal of detailed, relevant knowledge and understanding of two reasons for treating official statistics on crime carefully. There is evidence of appropriate and sustained sociological language throughout. The answer is of an appropriate length and shows very good understanding. The second reason is shorter but gains credit for using a range of sociological concepts and applying these accurately.

The second four marks are related to Application and the answer does relate closely to the question applying and explaining accurately the reliability of criminal statistics. This is a strong answer which has sufficient depth to do very well.

▶ **AO1+AO2 +AO3 question**

'Crime is caused by poverty.'
Do you agree with this view?   **(15 marks)**

The mark scheme allows 4 marks for AO1 Knowledge and Understanding and also 3 marks for AO2 Application, requiring the student to use the information skilfully to answer the question set. However, 7 marks are also available for evaluation, totalling 15 marks.

Students need to be careful not to give too much attention to knowledge and understanding and forget to apply and evaluate.

Weaker answer

I agree with this view as crime is caused by poverty as the poor do not have enough to survive. They then go out and steal things to get what they want. Merton said that people want the American Dream and turn to crime when they can't get it.

Criminals also start breaking the law when they form gangs and have their own ways of acting and things that they do. People who are in poverty tend to do this kind of thing.

Stronger answer

There is a lot of evidence to link poverty to crime and certainly areas with poverty are found to have higher crime rates. However, sociologists would think about other causes as having an effect on crime. This essay will also consider different theories and their reasons for crime. The essay will show that there are other causes, in addition to poverty.

New Right thinkers, like Charles Murray, would argue that poverty is a cause of crime rates being high. In particular, they would blame the culture of poverty. The culture of poverty is the set of ideas and values that people in poverty have developed. They have learned to live in poverty and have made a way of living which helps them deal with this. This includes crime, having no hope for the future or valuing education and the use of alcohol and drugs for cheap entertainment. Murray also blames the government for giving out benefits and making the poor give up as they know the government will help them out. This view suggests that crime is caused by poverty or at least the way of life of those in poverty.

A different view is that of Merton who blamed crime on anomie. He said that the pressure to succeed was so great that not everyone can succeed. He called this strain theory. Those who cannot succeed adapt in different ways. Some of these turn to innovation or crime in a bid to be successful. In this view it is not poverty but the values of society which influence crime.

Others have developed his ideas further and talked about the importance of subcultures in causing crime. Groups who cannot succeed create their own subculture which may involve criminal norms and values. In this view, associated with Cohen, the subcultures of society are the cause of crime. However, it is status frustration that causes the group to form the criminal subculture. The feelings of low status could be linked to poverty.

> The first answer has some points to make which show some partial knowledge of the connection between poverty and crime. It also suggests some knowledge of Merton's study but does not reveal detailed knowledge of this. There is limited evidence of sociological language and concepts. The explanation is partially developed at best although there is an attempt to link to the question title. Analysis and evaluation is limited.
>
> The answer could be improved with greater use of technical terms and a wider range of ideas.

Poverty itself is seen by Marxists as a result of the capitalist society we live in. The ruling class are greedy and grab the profits for themselves. It is inevitable that there will be those at the bottom of the pile living in poverty. They are also influenced by consumerism so that those in poverty may steal to get the things that they can't afford but that advertising makes them want.

On the other hand, Marxists also say that a lot of crime is committed by the ruling class and is hidden as they control the media, police and the courts. This sort of crime is not connected to poverty and is to do with ruling class greed. It is called corporate crime and committed by large companies. White-collar crime is also not related to poverty and is committed by people of a higher social class.

The second answer features detailed, relevant knowledge and understanding of a range of ideas relating to the idea of poverty as a cause of crime. There is evidence of appropriate and sustained sociological language and concepts are described in detail. Knowledge and understanding is applied and used to explain accurately the idea of poverty as a cause of crime. This answer has good analysis and some evaluation of the question. It could be improved by a final paragraph which pulls the answer together or alternatively, a stronger introductory paragraph which tells the examiner what the overall evaluation is.